comprehensive
mathematics practice

C. Oliver
Thomas Sumpter School, Scunthorpe

A. Ledsham
Head of Mathematics, The Abbey International College, Malvern Wells

R. Elvin
Formerly Head of Mathematics, Thomas Sumpter School, Scunthorpe

Oxford University Press

Oxford University Press, Walton Street, Oxford OX2 6DP

Oxford London Glasgow
New York Toronto Melbourne Auckland
Kuala Lumpur Singapore Hong Kong Tokyo
Delhi Bombay Calcutta Madras Karachi
Nairobi Dar es Salaam Cape Town

and associated companies in
Beirut Berlin Ibadan Mexico City Nicosia

Oxford is a trade mark of Oxford University Press

ISBN 19 833666 7
© C. Oliver, A. Ledsham, R. Elvin 1981
First published 1981
Reprinted 1981, 1982 (twice), 1983

Printed in Great Britain at the University Press, Oxford,
by Eric Buckley, Printer to the University

This series of six books is intended for the majority of pupils in the first years of secondary schooling. It provides a firm foundation in the mathematics needed at this level from which the pupils can proceed with confidence on a course to C.S.E. or G.C.E. 'O' Level. The books can be used either as a complete course or as a supplement to existing textbooks.

The material is arranged in sequential order. Each section includes brief teaching notes and worked examples followed by ample practice which is carefully graded. This ensures that most children gain the satisfaction of success as well as the experience of sufficient practice. Wherever possible, emphasis is laid on practical or topical aspects of the subject.

The numerical answers to the questions in all six books are provided in one separate book.

This arrangement of material in the books is intended to allow teachers to plan their own order of treatment to suit the aptitude and ability of a wide range of pupils: no specific scheme of work is presupposed. The series is designed to provide a relevant and lively course which should encourage the 'middle-of-the-road' pupils to gain confidence in their abilities and to master the fundamental processes so necessary for future mathematical success.

C.O.
A.H.C.L.
R.E.

CONTENTS

2347

The above number is in base 10. It consists of

    7 in the units column

    4 in the tens column

    3 in the hundreds column

and 2 in the thousands column.

The table below also shows this.

place value	$10 \times 10 \times 10$ thousands	10×10 hundreds	10 tens	1 units
digit	2	3	4	7

The place value of each column is 10 times greater than the column to its right.

If 2347 is in base 8, it consists of

    7 in the units column

    4 in the 8's column

    3 in the 64's column (8×8)

and 2 in the 512's column ($8 \times 8 \times 8$)

This is shown in the table below.

place value	$8 \times 8 \times 8$ 512's	8×8 64's	8 8's	1 units
digit	2	3	4	7

The place value of each column is 8 times greater than the column to its right.

Example 1

Put in table form 1011_{two} which is the base two number 1011.

place value	$2 \times 2 \times 2$ 8's	2×2 4's	2 2's	1 units
digit	1	0	1	1

Exercise 1

Put each of the following in table form.

1. 1325_{eight} 2. 2146_{eight} 3. 1754_{eight}

4. 3201_{eight} 5. 563_{eight} 6. 1324_{five}

7. 2412_{five} 8. 4023_{five} 9. 214_{five}

10. 1101_{two} 11. 1001_{two} 12. 11001_{two}

13. 11110_{two} 14. 10001_{two} 15. 3221_{four}

16. 1201_{four} 17. 332_{four} 18. 2112_{three}

19. 212_{three} 20. 21_{three}

The value in base 10 of a number written in a different base can be calculated by writing the number in table form.

Example 2

Find the value in base 10 of 231_{four}.

place value	4×4 16's	4 4's	1 units
digit	2	3	1
base 10 value	(2×16)	(3×4)	(1×1)

So, 231_{four} $= (2 \times 16) + (3 \times 4) + (1 \times 1)$

           $= 32 + 12 + 1$

           $= 45_{ten}$

Example 3

Find the value in base 10 of 10111_{two}.

place value	$2 \times 2 \times 2 \times 2$ 16's	$2 \times 2 \times 2$ 8's	2×2 4's	2 2's	1 units
digit	1	0	1	1	1
base 10 value	(1×16)	(0×8)	(1×4)	(1×2)	(1×1)

So, 10111_{two} $= (1 \times 16) + (0 \times 8) + (1 \times 4)$

             $+ (1 \times 2) + (1 \times 1)$

         $= 16 + 4 + 2 + 1$

         $= 23_{ten}$

Exercise 2

Find the value in base 10 of the following.

1. 1412_{five} 2. 1134_{five} 3. 1043_{five}

4. 2014_{five} 5. 342_{five} 6. 1110_{two}

7. 1010_{two} 8. 1111_{two} 9. 11001_{two}

10. 11010_{two} 11. 1122_{three} 12. 1021_{three}

13. 1202_{three} 14. 1132_{four} 15. 212_{four}

16. 223_{four}

For questions **17** to **26**, change the numbers to base 10 and find the 'odd answer out'.

17. a) 11110_{two} b) 112_{five} c) 132_{four}

18. a) 11000_{two} b) 101_{five} c) 122_{four}

19. a) 10101_{two} b) 34_{five} c) 111_{four}

20. a) 1101_{two} b) 23_{five} c) 33_{four}

21. a) 1102_{three} b) 123_{five} c) 47_{eight}

22. a) 1121_{three} b) 134_{five} c) 54_{eight}

23. a) 1220_{three} b) 203_{five} c) 65_{eight}

24. a) 1001_{three} b) 104_{five} c) 34_{eight}

25. a) 10011_{two} b) 122_{three} c) 103_{four}

26. a) 1011_{two} b) 101_{three} c) 23_{four}

A number in base 10 can be changed into a number in any other base.
Divide the base ten number by the new base repeatedly, as shown in Examples 4 and 5.
In each case, the remainders are read upwards to give the answer in the new base.

Example 4

Change 72_{ten} to base 8.

$$8\overline{)72}$$
$$8\overline{)\ 9}\ \ r\ 0\ (units)$$
$$8\overline{)\ 1}\ \ r\ 1\ (8's)$$
$$0\ \ r\ 1\ (8 \times 8's)$$

So $72_{ten} = 110_{eight}$

For a number in a base greater than 10, the symbol T is used for 10 units and the symbol E is used for 11 units.

Example 5

Change 119_{ten} to base 12.

$$12\overline{)119}$$
$$12\overline{)\ \ 9}\ \ r\ 11\ (units)$$
$$0\ \ r\ \ 9\ (12's)$$

So $119_{ten} = 9E_{twelve}$

Exercise 3

Change each number into the required base.

1. 395_{ten} to base 8   2. 366_{ten} to base 8

3. 452_{ten} to base 8   4. 496_{ten} to base 8

5. 321_{ten} to base 5   6. 284_{ten} to base 5

7. 227_{ten} to base 5   8. 375_{ten} to base 5

9. 35_{ten} to base 2   10. 42_{ten} to base 2

11. 29_{ten} to base 2   12. 20_{ten} to base 2

13. 75_{ten} to base 4   14. 96_{ten} to base 4

15. 53_{ten} to base 4   16. 34_{ten} to base 3

17. 25_{ten} to base 3   18. 385_{ten} to base 12

19. 279_{ten} to base 12   20. 178_{ten} to base 12

A fraction is turned into a decimal by dividing the numerator by the denominator.

e.g. $\frac{3}{4} = 3 \div 4 = 0.75$

Example 1

Change a) $\frac{5}{8}$ into a decimal fraction

b) $\frac{3}{40}$ into a decimal fraction

a) $\frac{5}{8} = 5 \div 8$
$\quad = 0.625$

$$\begin{array}{r} 0.625 \\ 8\overline{)5.000} \\ 4\,8 \\ \hline 20 \\ 16 \\ \hline 40 \\ 40 \\ \hline \end{array}$$

b) $\frac{3}{40} = 3 \div 40$
$\quad = 0.075$

$$\begin{array}{r} 0.075 \\ 40\overline{)3.000} \\ 2\,80 \\ \hline 200 \\ 200 \\ \hline \end{array}$$

Exercise 4

Change the following into decimal fractions.

1. $\frac{3}{8}$ 2. $\frac{3}{10}$ 3. $\frac{7}{10}$ 4. $\frac{2}{5}$

5. $\frac{4}{5}$ 6. $\frac{9}{20}$ 7. $\frac{11}{20}$ 8. $\frac{9}{40}$

9. $\frac{17}{40}$ 10. $\frac{7}{40}$ 11. $\frac{1}{40}$ 12. $\frac{11}{50}$

13. $\frac{41}{50}$ 14. $\frac{5}{16}$ 15. $\frac{9}{16}$

Sometimes the equivalent decimal fraction is a recurring decimal, i.e. a decimal in which a figure or a group of figures appears repeatedly.

e.g. $\frac{5}{9} = 0.555 \ldots$ or $0.\dot{5}$

$\frac{4}{11} = 0.3636 \ldots$ or $0.\dot{3}\dot{6}$

Exercise 5

Change the following into decimal fractions.

1. $\frac{2}{3}$ 2. $\frac{1}{3}$ 3. $\frac{5}{6}$ 4. $\frac{1}{6}$

5. $\frac{5}{12}$ 6. $\frac{7}{12}$ 7. $\frac{11}{12}$ 8. $\frac{1}{12}$

9. $\frac{4}{9}$ 10. $\frac{7}{9}$ 11. $\frac{1}{9}$ 12. $\frac{6}{11}$

13. $\frac{3}{11}$ 14. $\frac{7}{30}$ 15. $\frac{13}{30}$

Exercise 6

1. Peter weighs 31·6 kg. Find the weights of the following members of his family:
   a) Peter's father who is 3 times heavier than Peter.
   b) Peter's mother who is 28·8 kg lighter than his father.
   c) His baby sister Julie who weighs $\frac{1}{4}$ as much as his mother.

2. Wendy's folder contains 120 sheets of paper, each of weight 0·72 g. If the empty folder weighs 113·6 g, what is the total weight of her folder and the paper?

3. A large thermos flask holds sufficient coffee to exactly fill 2 large cups of capacity 0·24 litres and 4 smaller ones of capacity 0·13 litres. What is the capacity of the flask?

4. From the dimensions of the garage shown in the diagram below, find each of the following.
   a) The overall width of the garage.
   b) The height of the garage door.
   c) The area of the garage door.

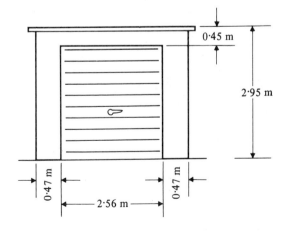

5. Look at the two set squares illustrated below.

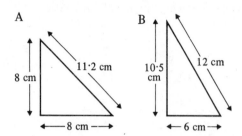

Find which one, A or B, has:
a) the longer perimeter and by how many centimetres,
b) the larger area and by how many square centimetres.

1.3 RATIO

The following exercise will help you to revise your knowledge of how to express a ratio in its simplest form.

Exercise 7

Give each of the following ratios in its simplest form.

1. 6 is to 10	**2.** 4 is to 10	**3.** 6 is to 20
4. 6 is to 9	**5.** 9 is to 15	**6.** 12 is to 16
7. 8 is to 20	**8.** 4 is to 20	**9.** 15 is to 40
10. 12 is to 30	**11.** 16 is to 40	**12.** 27 is to 36

13. £1·50 is to £2·00   **14.** £2·40 is to £6·00
15. £1·20 is to £4·00   **16.** £1·50 is to £6·00
17. £0·50 is to £4·00   **18.** 1 m 20 cm is to 3 m
19. 2 m 50 cm is to 3 m   **20.** 3 m 60 cm is to 4 m
21. 40 cm is to 2 m   **22.** 2 cm 4 mm is to 3 cm
23. 1 cm 5 mm is to 4 cm **24.** 1 cm 2 mm is to 6 cm
25. 5 mm is to 2 cm

If a quantity is to be shared between 2 people so that one gets twice as much as the other, it is shared in the ratio 2:1.

Example 1

Share a) £45 in the ratio 2:1
       b) 90 litres in the ratio 4:5:6

a) Total number of shares $= 2 + 1 = 3$

therefore one share $= £45 \div 3 = £15$

therefore the value of the first share
$$= £15 \times 2$$
$$= £30$$

and the value of the second share
$$= £15 \times 1$$
$$= £15$$

therefore the two amounts are £30 and £15.

Check that these two shares total £45.

b) Total number of shares $= 4 + 5 + 6 = 15$

therefore one share $= (90 \div 15)$ litres
$$= 6 \text{ litres}$$

therefore the first share $= (6 \times 4)$ litres
$$= 24 \text{ litres}$$

the second share $= (6 \times 5)$ litres
$$= 30 \text{ litres}$$

and the third share $= (6 \times 6)$ litres
$$= 36 \text{ litres}$$

therefore the three amounts are 24, 30 and 36 litres.

Check that these three shares total 90 litres.

Exercise 8

1. Share £48 in the ratio 2:1.
2. Share £60 in the ratio 3:1.
3. Share £80 in the ratio 4:1.
4. Share £91 in the ratio 6:1.
5. Share £70 in the ratio 3:2.
6. Share £120 in the ratio 5:3.
7. Share 112 ml of milk between the cat and her kitten in the ratio 4:3.
8. Share 162 ml of milk between the cat and the dog in the ratio 4:5.
9. Share 200 g of sweets between Anne and Nicola in the ratio 3:5.

10. Share 120 g of lemonade powder between William and David in the ratio 3:7.
11. Share £108 in the ratio 3:2:1.
12. Share £144 in the ratio 5:3:1.
13. Share £135 in the ratio 4:3:2.
14. Share £180 in the ratio 6:5:1;
15. Share £300 in the ratio 6:5:4.
16. Share 315 g of flour between Mrs. Smith, Mrs. Johnson and Mrs. Bates in the ratio 4:2:1.
17. Share 450 kg of soil between three gardeners in the ratio 4:5:6.
18. Share 1500 ml of paraffin between Mr. Brown, Mr. Jones and Mr. Simpson in the ratio 2:3:5.
19. A bottle containing 560 ml of lemonade, exactly fills three glasses belonging to Jill, Jane and Paul. If the capacities of the glasses are in the ratio of 3:5:6, how much lemonade does each child receive?

PAUL   JANE   JILL

20. A teacher shares out 50 sheets of paper between three pupils in the ratio 6:9:10. How many sheets does each pupil receive?

Example 2

A sum of money is shared in the ratio 2:3. If the smaller share is 50p, what is the larger share?

  50p is equal to 2 shares,
so 25p is equal to 1 share,

therefore, the larger share = 25p X 3 = 75p

Check that the two shares are in the ratio 2:3.

Exercise 9

1. A sum of money is shared in the ratio 2:3. If the smaller share is 30p, what is the larger share?
2. A sum of money is shared in the ratio 2:5. If the smaller share is 16p, what is the larger share?
3. A sum of money is shared in the ratio 4:5. If the smaller share is 36p, what is the larger share? How much money was shared out?
4. A sum of money is shared in the ratio 3:7. If the smaller share is £12, what is the larger share? How much money was shared out?
5. A sum of money is shared in the ratio 5:8. If the smaller share is £20, what is the larger share? How much money was shared out?
6. A sum of money is shared out in the ratio 2:3:5. If the smallest share is £10, what are the other two shares?
7. A sum of money is shared out in the ratio 3:5:7. If the smallest share is £9, what are the other two shares?
8. A sum of money is shared out in the ratio 5:6:9. If the smallest share is 25p, what are the other two shares? How much money was shared out altogether?
9. At a bread shop the prices of a white and a brown loaf are in the ratio of 5:6. If a white loaf costs 30p, what is the price of a brown loaf?
10. The heights of two sisters Lynn and Christine are in the ratio of 4:5. If Lynn is 120 cm tall, how tall is Christine?
11. The weights of two brothers Martin and Richard are in the ratio of 3:4. If Martin's weight is 45 kg, how much does Richard weigh?
12. A thermos flask can exactly fill two cups whose capacities are in the ratio of 3:5. If the smaller one has a capacity of 150 ml, what is the capacity of the larger one? What is the capacity of the flask?
13. In class 3A the ratio of boys to girls is 6:7. If there are 12 boys in the class, find a) the number of girls in the class and b) the number of pupils in the class altogether.
14. A long, thin piece of wood is cut into two pieces, the ratio of whose lengths is 9:11. If the shorter piece is 45 cm long, what is the length of the longer piece? What was the length of the original piece?

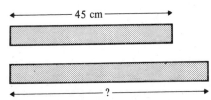

15. Some sweets are shared between Tom, Bill and Mary in the ratio 2:3:4. If Tom has 100 g, what weight has a) Bill and b) Mary? What total weight of sweets was shared out?
16. The boys in class 4B have three sports options, cross-country, rugby and football. If they choose in the respective ratio 2:5:8 and 4 choose cross-country, how many choose a) rugby and b) football. How many boys are there in the class altogether?
17. The girls in class 5A have three sports options, squash, netball and hockey. If they choose in the respective ratio 3:4:7 and 6 choose squash, how many choose a) netball and b) hockey? How many girls are there in the class altogether?
18. A sum of money is shared in the ratio 5:3. If 30p is the larger share, what is the smaller share?
19. A sum of money is shared in the ratio 7:2. If £28 is the larger share, what is the smaller share? How much money was shared out?
20. The ages of two sisters Anne and Margaret are in the ratio of 3:2. If Anne is 12 years old, how old is Margaret?

Example 3

a) If 3 kg of apples cost 99p, what would 5 kg cost?
b) If 12 eggs cost 60p, how many eggs could be bought for 45p?

a) If 3 kg of apples cost 99p,
   then 1 kg of apples cost $99 \div 3 = 33p$

   therefore 5 kg costs $33 \times 5 = 165p = £1 \cdot 65$

b) If 12 eggs cost 60p,
   then 1 egg costs $60 \div 12 = 5p$

   therefore, the number of eggs for 45p
   is $45 \div 5 = 9$.

Exercise 10

1. If 5 kg of potatoes cost 90p, what is the cost of 3 kg?
2. If 6 litres of paraffin cost 96p, what is the cost of 4 litres?
3. If 20 cigarettes cost 60p, what is the cost of 50?
4. If it takes me 45 minutes to walk 5 km, how long will it take me to walk a) 9 km and b) 4 km?
5. If 12 m² of carpet cost £60, find the cost of a) 5 m² and b) 8 m².
6. If 5 kg of bananas cost £2·40, find the cost of 2 kg
7. If 4 kg of tomatoes cost £3·60, find the cost of 3 kg.
8. If 6 kg of apples cost £1·92, find the cost of a) 4 kg and b) 5 kg.
9. If 5 kg of pears cost £1·80, find the cost of a) 3 kg and b) 4 kg.
10. If 5 m of curtain track cost £2, find the cost of a) 3 m and b) 8 m.
11. If 5 m of dress cloth cost £7, find the cost of a) 4 m and b) 12 m.
12. If 10 m of a certain kind of electric wire cost £5, find the cost of a) 3 m and b) 7 m.
13. If 10 m² of linoleum cost £12, find the cost of a) 3 m², b) 8 m² and c) 12 m².
14. If 10 tonnes of garden soil cost £75, find the cost of a) 3 tonnes, b) 4 tonnes and c) 12 tonnes.
15. If 20 litres of petrol cost £6, find the cost of a) 8 litres, b) 12 litres and c) 30 litres.
16. If 8 oranges cost 96p, how many can be bought for 60p.
17. If 5 grapefruits cost 80p, how many can be bought for 48p?
18. If 6 eggs cost 36p, how many can be bought for 90p?
19. If 5 bread buns cost 30p, how many can be bought for a) 18p, b) 48p?
20. If 5 doughnuts cost 60p, how many can be bought for a) 24p, b) 84p.
21. If 6 packets of crisps cost 48p, how many packets can be bought for a) 32p, b) 72p?
22. If 6 pencils cost 54p, how many can be bought for a) 36p, b) 90p?
23. If 12 Christmas cards cost 84p, how many can be bought for a) 35p, b) 56p?
24. If 30 envelopes cost 60p, how many can be bought for a) 50p, b) 90p?
25. If 4 bars of chocolate cost 60p, how many can be bought for a) 45p, b) £1·50?
26. If 5 calculator batteries cost £1·50, how many can be bought for a) 90p, b) £2·10?
27. If 10 bars of soap cost £1·20, how many can be bought for a) 48p, b) 84p, c) £1·08?
28. If 10 cans of lemonade cost £2, how many cans can be bought for a) 60p, b) £1·60, c) £2·80?
29. If 60 brass screws cost £1·80, how many can be bought for a) 45p, b) £1·50?
30. If 12 bathroom tiles cost £3·60, how many can be bought for a) £2·40, b) £6?

A percentage of a quantity can be found by first changing the percentage into a common fraction and then calculating this fraction of the quantity.

Example 1

Find:
a) 15% of £500   b) 66% of 250 g
c) $12\frac{1}{2}$% of 1 m 60 cm

a) 15% as a fraction $= \frac{15}{100}$,

This fraction of £500 $= \frac{15}{100} \times \frac{500^{5}}{1} = £75$

b) 66% as a fraction $= \frac{66}{100}$,

This fraction of 250 g $= \frac{66^{33}}{100} \times \frac{250^{5}}{1}$

$= 165$ g

c) $12\frac{1}{2}$% as a fraction $= \frac{12\frac{1}{2}}{100} = \frac{25}{200}$

This fraction of 1 m 60 cm (or 160 cm) $= \frac{25}{200} \times \frac{160^{20}}{1}$

$= 20$ cm

Exercise 11

Find:

1. 8% of £500
2. 5% of £900
3. 6% of 400 g
4. 3% of £1200
5. 20% of £60
6. 60% of £90
7. 50% of 30 cm
8. 40% of £120
9. 80% of £110
10. 40% of £25
11. 60% of £15
12. 20% of 75 cm
13. 80% of 35 cm
14. 25% of £96
15. 75% of £28
16. 75% of £64
17. 35% of £60
18. 45% of 80 cm
19. 15% of 120 g
20. 40% of £1·50
21. 60% of £1·20
22. 80% of 1 m 10 cm
23. 20% of £3·50
24. 60% of £2·50

25. 40% of £3·20
26. 25% of £1·80
27. 75% of 1 m 20 cm
28. 75% of 1 kg
29. $12\frac{1}{2}$% of £72
30. $12\frac{1}{2}$% of £4·80

One quantity can be written as a percentage of another quantity, provided each quantity is written in the same units.
First put one quantity as a fraction of the other. Then multiply this fraction by 100.

Example 2

Find:
a) 10 cm as a percentage of 50 cm,
b) £1·50 as a percentage of £5,
c) 250 g as a percentage of 2 kg.

a) 10 as a fraction of 50 $= \frac{10}{50}$,

Therefore, 10 as a percentage of 50 $= \frac{10}{50} \times \frac{100^{2}}{1}$%

$= 20$%

b) £1·50 as a fraction of £5 $= \frac{1·50}{5·00} = \frac{150}{500}$

Therefore, £1·50 as a percentage of £5 $= \frac{150^{30}}{500} \times \frac{100^{1}}{1}$%

$= 30$%

c) 250 g as a fraction of 2 kg (or 2000 g) $= \frac{250}{2000}$

Therefore, 250 g as a percentage of 2 kg $= \frac{250^{25}}{2000} \times \frac{100^{1}}{1}$%

$= \frac{25}{2}$% $= 12\frac{1}{2}$%

Exercise 12

Find:

1. £72 as a percentage of £800
2. £42 as a percentage of £600
3. 56 g as a percentage of 700 g
4. £66 as a percentage of £1100
5. £35 as a percentage of £50
6. £27 as a percentage of £90
7. £54 as a percentage of £60
8. 32 cm as a percentage of 80 cm
9. 24 cm as a percentage of 30 cm
10. £45 as a percentage of £75
11. £18 as a percentage of £45
12. £100 as a percentage of £125
13. £21 as a percentage of £105
14. £28 as a percentage of £80
15. 66 g as a percentage of 120 g
16. £24 as a percentage of £160
17. 27 cm as a percentage of 60 cm
18. 54 cm as a percentage of 72 cm
19. £27 as a percentage of £108
20. £1·20 as a percentage of £1·50
21. £1·40 as a percentage of £3·50
22. 1 m 44 cm as a percentage of 2 m 40 cm
23. £2 as a percentage of £2·50
24. 72p as a percentage of £1·80
25. 96p as a percentage of £1·20
26. 84p as a percentage of £1·40
27. 54 cm as a percentage of 2 m 70 cm
28. 35p as a percentage of £1·40
29. £1·80 as a percentage of £2·40
30. 50 cm as a percentage of 4 m

Example 3

In a school of 1400 pupils, 45% of them are boys.

Find:

a) the number of boys in the school
b) the percentage of the pupils who stay for lunch if 770 of them do so.

a) Number of boys = 45% of 1400

$$= \frac{45}{100_1} \times \frac{1400^{14}}{1}$$

$$= 45 \times 14 = 630$$

b) Fraction who stay $= \dfrac{770}{1400}$

Therefore, the percentage who stay $= \dfrac{\overset{110}{\cancel{770}}}{\underset{\underset{2}{14}}{\cancel{1400}}} \times \dfrac{\overset{1}{\cancel{100}}}{1} \%$

$$= \frac{110}{2}\% = 55\%$$

Exercise 13

1. A football club has 25 players, but only 60% of them have ever played for the first team. Find the number who have played for the first team.
2. It takes me 45 minutes to get to school and I spend 80% of that time travelling on the bus. How long does my bus journey last?
3. A room has an area of 30 m² and a carpet covers 90% of this area. Find the area of the carpet.
4. A farmer has 40 sheep and 35% of them are black. Find the number of black sheep.
5. A car's petrol tank can hold 36 litres. How many litres are there in it if it is 75% full?
6. There are 32 boys in class 5A and one day $12\frac{1}{2}\%$ of them are absent. Find the number who are absent.
7. At 3 p.m. a newspaper seller is given 350 papers and by 5 p.m. he has sold 40% of them. Find the number that he has sold by 5 p.m.
8. A match box had 50 matches inside when it was bought, but only 70% of them are left. How many matches have been used?
9. There are 20 boys in class 1B and they have three sports options to choose from. If 25% choose athletics, 35% choose swimming and 40% choose cricket, find the number who choose each of the three sports.
10. At Northgate School there are 750 pupils. The percentage absent on each day of a certain week is shown below.

Monday	8%	Thursday	2%
Tuesday	10%	Friday	4%
Wednesday	6%		

    Find the number absent on each day.
11. There are 20 eggs in a fridge and 6 of them are brown. Find the percentage which are brown.
12. A passage has an area of 25 m² and there is a carpet on its floor which has an area of 20 m². What percentage of the floor's area is covered by the carpet?

13. An examination is marked out of 120 and one girl gets 84 marks. Find her mark as a percentage.
14. 60 pupils are entered for an examination and 45 of them pass. Find the percentage who pass.
15. A factory employs 160 workers and 72 of them travel to work by bus. Find the percentage who use the bus.
16. There are 24 girls in class 2B and one day 18 of them are present. Find the percentage who are present.
17. At a football match a programme seller is supplied with 1200 programmes and he sells 1080. What percentage of them does he sell?
18. 10 m of wood is used to make the window frame illustrated. What percentage of the wood is used?

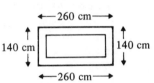

19. There are 30 girls in class 4C and they have four sports options to choose from. If 12 choose tennis, 9 choose swimming, 3 choose rounders and 6 choose athletics, find the percentage who choose each sport.
20. At Manor Grange School there are 450 pupils. The number absent on each day of a certain week is shown below.

Monday	27	Thursday	36
Tuesday	18	Friday	54
Wednesday	45		

Find the percentage who are absent on each day.

1.5 AVERAGES

Reminder

The average of a set of data is found as follows.

$$\text{average} = \frac{\text{sum of all items}}{\text{total number of items}}$$

Example 1

Four bus journeys from Wolverhampton to Shrewsbury took the following times.
1 h 22 min, 1 h 24 min, 1 hr 32 min,
1 h 30 min.
Find the average journey time.

The times are 82 min, 84 min, 92 min, and 90 min.

$$\text{Average time} = \frac{\text{sum of times}}{\text{no. of journeys}}$$

$$= \frac{82 + 84 + 92 + 90}{4}$$

$$= \frac{348}{4} = 87 \text{ min}$$

$$= 1 \text{ hr } 27 \text{ min}$$

Exercise 14

Find the average in questions **1** to **8**.

1. 13 min, 3 min, 2 min, 10 min, 22 min
2. 53 min, 48 min, 52 min, 49 min, 53 min
3. 51 s, 54 s, 55 s, 57 s, 53 s
4. 2 min 4 s, 2 min 6 s, 2 min 7 s, 2 min 8 s, 2 min 10 s
5. 1 h 6 min, 1 h 8 min, 1 h 5 min, 1 h 9 min
6. 4 h 2 min, 4 h 15 min, 4 h 24 min, 4 h 11 min
7. 30 days, 31 days, 30 days, 31 days, 30 days, 28 days
8. 1 year 6 months, 1 year 8 months, 1 year 10 months, 1 year 4 months.
9. On five weekday nights John found that his homework took the following times.

Mon.	1 h 40 min	Thu.	1 h 35 min
Tue.	1 h 45 min	Fri.	1 h 5 min
Wed.	1 h 25 min		

   Find the average time that he spent on his homework.
10. Five train journeys from London to Liverpool took the following times.

    | 2 h 28 min | 2 h 30 min |
    | 2 h 33 min | 2 h 38 min |
    | 2 h 41 min | |

    Find the average time.

11. A 1500 metre runner completes four races in the following times.

4 min 15 s   4 min 12 s
4 min 20 s   4 min 5 s

Find his average time.

12. Four football matches all start at 3 p.m. and end at the following times.

4.45 p.m.   4.38 p.m.
4.42 p.m.   4.43 p.m.

Find the average start-to-finish time of the matches.

If the average of a set of numbers is known, then the sum of these numbers can be calculated.
Multiply the average by the number of items in the set.

Example 2

The average of a set of six numbers is 12. What is their sum?

Sum of the numbers = 12 × 6 = 72

Example 3

The average weekly wage of five paper boys is £3·84. How much do they earn altogether in one week?

Total earnings = £3·84 × 5 = £19·20

Exercise 15

1. A newspaper seller works six evenings per week. If he sold an average of 325 papers an evening in one week, find the total number that he sold.
2. An ice cream seller works seven days a week. If he sold an average of 245 cornets per day during a week, find the total number that he sold.
3. On average I use up a tube of toothpaste every 35 days. For how many weeks can I expect 6 tubes to last?
4. At Holly Grove School the average number of pupils per class is 25. If there are 24 classes, how many pupils are there in the school altogether?
5. On average I find that I can drive my car for a distance of 15 km on 1 litre of petrol. How far could I expect to travel on a full tank of petrol if the tank's capacity is 32 litres?

6. Nine men, whose average weight is 75 kg, are travelling in a minibus of weight 3275 kg. The bus arrives at a bridge where there is a notice saying 'Maximum permitted load 4 tonnes'. Is it safe for the bus to cross?
7. In Manchester there was an average of 8·5 wet days per month during 1979. How many wet days were there during the whole year?
8. Over a career lasting 20 seasons, a footballer made an average number of 1·8 appearances for England per season. How many times did he play for England altogether?
9. A cricketer played for one club for 25 seasons. His average number of centuries per season was 1·6. How many centuries did he make altogether?
10. A small firm, which operates 5 days a week, spent an average amount of 54p per day on postal charges during a certain week. How much was spent on postal charges for the whole week?
11. During the four weeks of February an errand boy's average wage was £3·75. How much did he earn over the whole month?
12. A waitress, who works 6 days a week, made an average of £1·35 a day in tips during a certain week. How much did she make in tips over the whole week?
13. Last year my average quarterly electricity bill was £30·45. What was my electricity bill for the whole year?
14. One week Jane found that she spent an average time of 1 h 30 min on her homework each night from Monday to Friday inclusive. How much time did she spend on her homework during that week altogether?
15. One week a newspaper boy, who works 6 days a week, found that it took him an average time of 45 minutes per day to complete his round. How much time did he spend delivering papers over the whole week?

Example 4

A set of numbers has an average of 36 and a sum of 144. How many numbers are there in the set?

$$\text{Number in set} = \frac{\text{total}}{\text{average}} = \frac{144}{36} = 4$$

Exercise 16

1. The average weight of a group of men is 75 kg. If their total weight is 600 kg, how many men are there in the group?
2. The average weight of a group of women is 55 kg. If their total weight is 330 kg, how many women are there in the group?
3. The average weight of a group of boys is 46 kg. If their total weight is 230 kg, how many boys are there in the group?
4. A footballer scored a total of 270 goals throughout his playing career and his average per season was 15 goals. For how many seasons did his career last?
5. A clerk finds that he uses, on average, 50 staples per day. If he has a box containing 3500 staples, how many weeks can he expect them to last?
6. Vitamin pills are sold in bottles which contain an average number of 250 pills. How many bottles would be required for 3000 pills?

7. I buy a new car and use it to drive an average distance of 1250 km per month. How long will it be before the distanceometer reads 20 000 km?
8. On filling my pen I use, on average, 0·4 ml of ink. How many times can I expect to fill my pen from a full bottle containing 60 ml of ink?
9. A certain kind of tree is known to grow at an average rate of 5 cm per month. After how many years would a newly planted seed produce a tree of height 3 metres?
10. On average I find that my torch needs a new battery every 73 days. If I want sufficient batteries to last 2 years how many must I buy?
11. On average I use one bar of soap every 28 days. If I want sufficient soap to last 20 weeks, how many bars must I buy?
12. The average weight of a certain kind of loaf of bread is 350 g. A baker has a full tray of such loaves which weighs 12 kg. If the empty tray weighs 5 kg, how many loaves does the tray contain?

REVISION EXERCISE A

Find the 'odd answer out'.

1. a) 5% of £300
   b) 20% of £80
   c) 30% of £50
2. a) 6% of £400
   b) 30% of £80
   c) 40% of £70
3. a) 8% of £400
   b) 12% of £300
   c) 40% of £90

4. a) 9% of 500 m
   b) 8% of 600 m
   c) 12% of 400 m
5. a) 15% of 400 m
   b) 90% of 70 m
   c) 80% of 75 m
6. a) 60% of 125 g
   b) 50% of 150 g
   c) 40% of 180 g

7. a) 25% of 140 ml
   b) 20% of 150 ml
   c) 15% of 200 ml
8. a) 60% of £1·20
   b) 50% of £1·40
   c) 80% of 90p
9. a) 20% of 2 m 70 cm
   b) 25% of 2 m 24 cm
   c) 5% of 10 m 80 cm

10. a) 25% of £5·00
    b) 30% of £4·20
    c) 5% of £25·20

Find the 'odd answer out' by changing each to a percentage.

11. a) £45 of £500
    b) £48 of £600
    c) £4 of £50
12. a) £15 of £300
    b) £24 of £400
    c) £50 of £1000
13. a) £36 of £900
    b) £28 of £700
    c) £60 of £1200

14. a) 30 m of 120 m
    b) 18 m of 90 m
    c) 40 m of 200 m
15. a) 200 m of 250 m
    b) 225 m of 300 m
    c) 60 m of 75 m
16. a) 60 ml of 150 ml
    b) 90 ml of 200 ml
    c) 50 ml of 125 ml

17. a) 12 g of 80 g
    b) 45 g of 300 g
    c) 15 g of 75 g
18. a) £1·05 of £3·50
    b) £1·20 of £4·80
    c) £1·50 of £6·00
19. a) 84p of £1·20
    b) 96p of £1·28
    c) £1·08 of £1·44

20. a) 2 m 70 cm of 4 m 50 cm
    b) 1 m 75 cm of 3 m 50 cm
    c) 1 m 80 cm of 3 m

21. One year at Willow Bank School there was a double success when the boys won a football trophy and the girls won a netball trophy. Both teams competed in a six-round contest and their results are shown below.

Football team

1st round	Willow Bank	5	West Park	1
2nd round	Willow Bank	4	Oak Vale	3
3rd round	Willow Bank	2	Southmead	1
4th round	Willow Bank	3	Lea Road	2
Semi-final	Willow Bank	4	Fairfield	2
Final	Willow Bank	6	Holly Grange	3

Netball team

1st round	Willow Bank	10	Fairfield	5
2nd round	Willow Bank	12	Southmead	8
3rd round	Willow Bank	15	Manor Lane	11
4th round	Willow Bank	16	Oak Vale	7
Semi-final	Willow Bank	20	Grove Street	12
Final	Willow Bank	11	Beech Avenue	5

Find: a) the average number of goals scored per match by the football team.
  b) the average number of goals scored per match against the football team.
  c) the average number of goals scored per match by the netball team.
  d) the average number of goals scored per match against the netball team.

22. In a small town there is a local bus service which calls at only three stops between the bus station and the terminus in Fairfield Estate. The fare table is shown below.

Bus Station

10p	High Street			
20p	10p	Park Road		
20p.	15p	10p	St. Peter's Church	
25p	20p	15p	10p	Fairfield Estate

One day a bus leaves the bus station and passengers join as follows:

Three board at the Bus Station, 2 for Fairfield Estate and 1 for Park Road.
Ten board in the High Street, 4 for Fairfield Estate, 2 for St. Peter's Church and 4 for Park Road.
Six board at Park Road, 2 for Fairfield Estate and 4 for St. Peter's Church.
One passenger for Fairfield Estate boards at St. Peter's Church.

Find: a) the total number of passengers who board the bus.
  b) the total amount that they pay in fares.
  c) the average fare paid per passenger.

23. At a preparatory school for boys there are five classes and four houses. The table shows the full details.

	Number in North house	Number in South house	Number in East house	Number in West house
Class 1	7	4	6	3
Class 2	2	5	3	2
Class 3	6	3	4	3
Class 4	5	4	3	8
Class 5	2	3	4	3

Find: a) the number of boys in each of the five classes.
  b) the total number of boys in the school.
  c) the percentage of the total number in each of the five classes.

24. A small school for girls has five classes and the girls can choose from four sports options. The table below shows how many girls choose each of these options.

	Hockey	Netball	Badminton	Squash
Class 1	4	6	6	8
Class 2	9	8	4	7
Class 3	7	9	5	5
Class 4	6	7	5	4
Class 5	4	6	4	6

Find: a) the total number of girls that choose each option.
      b) the total number of girls in the school.
      c) the percentage of the total number who choose each option.
      d) the number of girls in each of the five classes.
      e) the average number of girls per class

25. The table below shows the results of the Summer Term tests for Class 1B.

	History (out of 10)	Geography (out of 10)	Craft (out of 20)	Science (out of 20)	English (out of 25)	Mathematics (out of 50)
Peter	5	6	14	10	15	35
William	7	4	7	11	10	30
John	8	5	13	15	20	35
David	3	2	10	12	10	20
Michael	8	6	15	17	15	45
Anne	6	2	11	9	15	15
Jane	7	8	13	19	20	45
Margaret	6	7	10	12	10	25
Julie	4	3	7	11	5	15
Susan	8	7	9	13	15	35

Find: a) all the above marks as percentages.
      b) the average percentage mark for each pupil.

26. The wood required for making the gate illustrated is only sold in metre lengths.

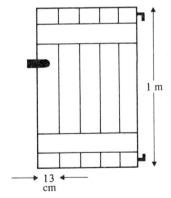

Find: a) the number of metre lengths required.
      b) the length of wood which has to be wasted.
      c) the percentage of the total length which has to be wasted.

1 m

13 cm

Reminder

If two parallel lines are cut by a transversal, then

a) Alternate angles are equal

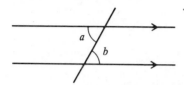

$\hat{a} = \hat{b}$ as they are alternate angles.

b) Corresponding angles are equal

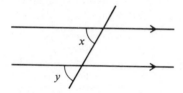

$\hat{x} = \hat{y}$ as they are corresponding angles.

c) Vertically opposite angles are equal

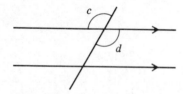

$\hat{c} = \hat{d}$ as they are vertically opposite angles.

d) Allied angles are supplementary, i.e. their sum is 180°.

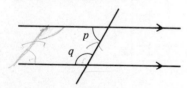

$\hat{p} + \hat{q} = 180°$ as they are allied angles.

e) Adjacent angles are supplementary

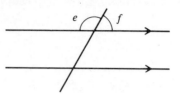

$\hat{e} + \hat{f} = 180°$ as they are adjacent angles.

Exercise 17

1. Copy the drawings and colour in all the equal angles in each pattern. You will need two different colours.

a)

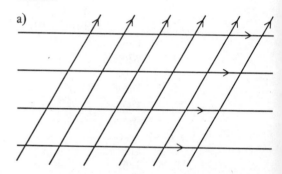

b)

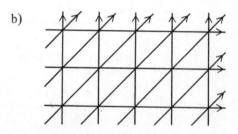

2. Copy and complete the following statements.
   a) Alternate angles are . . .
   b) Corresponding angles are . . .
   c) Adjacent angles are . . .
   d) Allied angles are . . .
   e) Vertically opposite angles are . . .

3. Look at the diagrams below, then copy and complete the statements.

a)

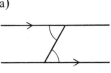

b)

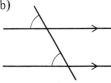

c)

d)

e)

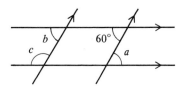

Corresponding angles are show in diagram . . .
Allied angles are shown in diagram . . .
Vertically opposite angles are shown in diagram . . .
Adjacent angles are shown in diagram . . .
Alternate angles are shown in diagram . . .

Example 1

Find the size of the lettered angles in the diagram, giving reasons.

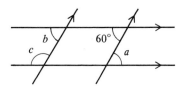

a) $\hat{a}$ and $60°$ are equal because they are alternate angles.

$\hat{a} = 60°$

b) $\hat{b}$ and $60°$ are equal because they are corresponding angles.

$\hat{b} = 60°$

c) $\hat{b}$ and $\hat{c}$ are supplementary because they are allied angles.

$\hat{b} + \hat{c} = 180°$

So $60° + \hat{c} = 180°$

$\hat{c} = 120°$

Exercise 18

Find the size of each lettered angle, giving reasons.

1.

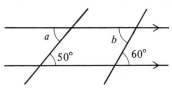

2.

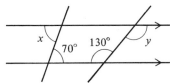

3.

4.

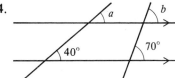

5.

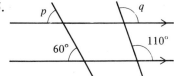

6.

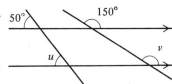

7.

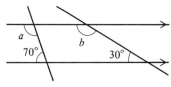

8.

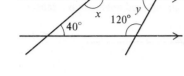

9.

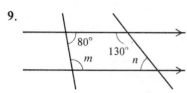

10.

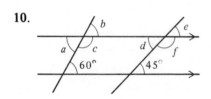

11.

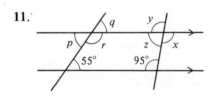

12.

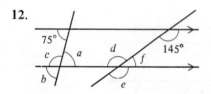

Example 2

State whether or not the lines AB and CD are parallel, giving reasons.

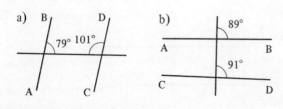

a) $79° + 101° = 180°$

So AB is parallel to CD because the allied angles are supplementary.

b) AB is not parallel to CD because the 'corresponding angles' of 91° and 89° are not equal.

Exercise 19

For each question state whether or not the lines AB and CD are parallel, giving reasons.

1.

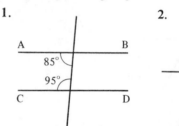

2.

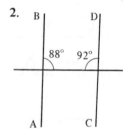

3.

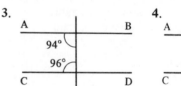

4.

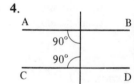

5.

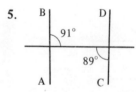

6.

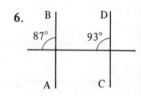

7.

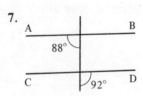

8.

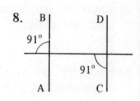

9.

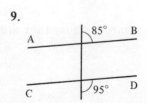

10.

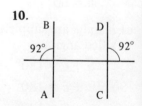

A quadrilateral is a closed figure with four sides and four angles. The sum of these four angles is 360°.

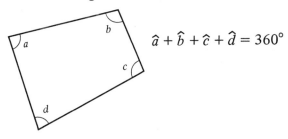

$$\hat{a} + \hat{b} + \hat{c} + \hat{d} = 360°$$

Exercise 20

Carefully copy these special quadrilaterals: you may find it easier to trace them.

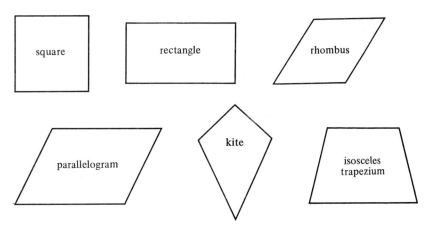

Then answer the following questions for each of the six shapes.

1. Are all the sides the same length?
2. Are the opposite sides equal?
3. Are the adjacent sides equal?
4. Are the opposite sides parallel?
5. Are all the angles right angles?
6. Are the opposite angles the same size?
7. Are the diagonals the same length?
8. Do the diagonals cut each other at right angles?
9. Do the diagonals cut each other at right angles?
10. Is the shape symmetrical? If so, state:
    a) the number of lines of symmetry
    b) the order of rotational symmetry (if any).

Exercise 21

Copy and complete the following statements.

1. A *square* has . . . sides. It has . . . angles and each angle is . . .°. Each of its four sides are . . . and the opposite sides are . . . It has . . . lines of symmetry.
The diagonals are . . . and bisect each other at . . . angles.

2. A *rectangle* has . . . sides. It has . . . angles and each angle is . . .°. The opposite sides are . . . and . . . and it has . . . lines of symmetry.
The diagonals are . . .

3. A *rhombus* has . . . sides and . . . angles. All the sides are . . . and the opposite sides are . . . The . . . angles are equal and it has . . . lines of symmetry.
The diagonals . . . each other at . . . angles.

4. A *parallelogram* has . . . sides and . . . angles. The opposite sides are . . . and . . . The . . . angles are equal. It has . . . lines of symmetry.

5. A *kite* has . . . sides and . . . angles. There are . . . pairs of . . . sides but the opposite sides are . . . equal. It has . . . . . . of symmetry.
The diagonals cross and produce four . . . angles at this point.

6. An *isosceles trapezium* has . . . sides and . . . angles. One pair of opposite sides are . . . and one pair of opposite sides are . . . It has . . . . . . of symmetry.
The diagonals are . . .

Exercise 22

1. Look at the two right-angled triangles in the illustration.

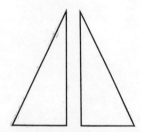

Draw a diagram to show how the pair can be arranged to form:
a) a rectangle,
b) a parallelogram,
c) a kite.

2. Look at the two isosceles triangles in the illustration.

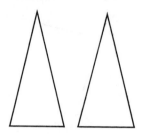

Draw a diagram to show how the pair can be arranged to form:
a) a parallelogram,
b) a rhombus,
c) a kite.

3. Look at the four right-angled triangles in the illustration.

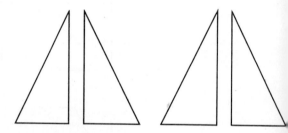

Draw a diagram to show how they can be arranged to form:
a) a rectangle,
b) a rhombus,
c) a parallelogram,
d) an isosceles trapezium.

4. Draw diagrams to show how:
a) Two equilateral triangles can form a rhombus.
b) Three equilateral triangles can form an isosceles trapezium.
c) Four equilateral triangles can form a parallelogram.
d) Four right-angled isosceles triangles can form a square.

A *polygon* is a plane figure with three or more straight sides.

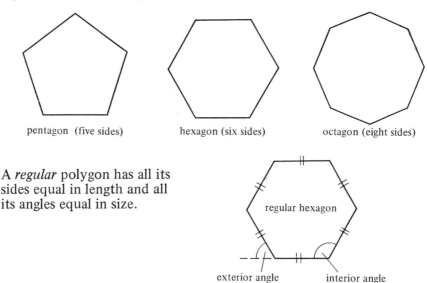

pentagon (five sides)   hexagon (six sides)   octagon (eight sides)

A *regular* polygon has all its
sides equal in length and all
its angles equal in size.

regular hexagon

exterior angle   interior angle

Example 1

Look at the diagram above of a regular hexagon and then answer the
following questions about it.

a) How many equal interior angles are there?
b) How many diagonals can be drawn from one vertex, and how many
   triangles are so formed?
c) What is the sum of the interior angles?
d) What is the size of any one of these interior angles?

a) There are 6 equal interior angles.
b) Three diagonals can be drawn
   from one vertex; and 4 triangles
   are formed.
c) The sum of the interior angles
   is the sum of the angles in the
   4 triangles.

$$4 \times 180° = 720°$$

d) Each of the interior angles is $720° \div 6 = 120°$

Exercise 23

Look at these regular polygons.

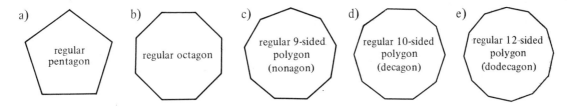

a) regular pentagon

b) regular octagon

c) regular 9-sided polygon (nonagon)

d) regular 10-sided polygon (decagon)

e) regular 12-sided polygon (dodecagon)

Then answer the following questions for all five shapes.

1. How many equal interior angles does the polygon have?
2. How many diagonals can be drawn from one vertex, and how many triangles are so formed?
3. What is the sum of the interior angles?
4. What is the size of any one of the interior angles?

Example 2

Look at the diagram opposite of a regular octagon, and then answer the following questions.

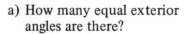

a) How many equal exterior angles are there?
b) What is the sum of the exterior angles?
c) What is the size of one of the exterior angles?
d) What is the sum of an exterior angle and an interior angle?

a) There are 8 equal exterior angles.
b) The sum of the exterior angles is equal to 360°.
c) The size of one exterior angle is 360° ÷ 8 = 45°.
d) The exterior angle and the interior angle are on a straight line, so their sum is 180°.

Exercise 24

Look at these regular polygons.

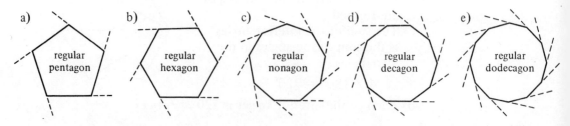

a) regular pentagon
b) regular hexagon
c) regular nonagon
d) regular decagon
e) regular dodecagon

Then answer the following questions for all five shapes.

1. How many equal exterior angles does the polygon have?
2. What is the sum of the exterior angles?
3. What is the size of any one of the equal exterior angles?
4. What is the sum of an exterior and an interior angle?

Example 3

a) ABCDEF is a regular hexagon.
Describe the figures:
i) ABC   ii) ACD   iii) ADEF

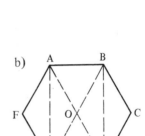

a)

i) ABC is an isosceles
   triangle.
ii) ACD is a right-angled
    triangle.
iii) ADEF is an isosceles
     trapezium.

b) O is the centre of a regular
hexagon ABCDEF. Describe
the figures:
i) AOB   ii) AOEF   iii) BDEA

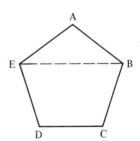

b)

i) AOB is an equilateral
   triangle.
ii) AOEF is a rhombus.
iii) BDEA is a rectangle.

Exercise 25

1. ABCDEF is a regular pentagon.
   Describe the figures:
   i) ABE   ii) EBCD

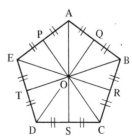

2. ABCDEF is a regular pentagon
   and O is its centre. If P, Q, R, S
   and T are the mid-points of the
   sides, describe the figures:
   i) DOC   ii) AQOP   iii) TOSD

3. ABCDEFGH is a regular octagon.
   Describe the figures:
      i) ACEG   ii) ACQP
     iii) ABCO   iv) ABFG
       v) OQE   vi) GOE
     vii) AGH

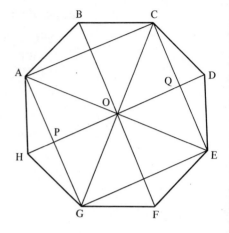

4. ABCDEFGHI is a regular nonagon.
   Describe the figures:
      i) ABI
     ii) BEFI
     iii) BCDE

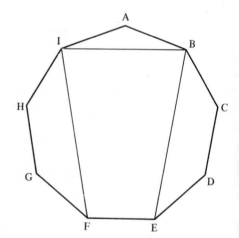

5. ABCDEFGHI is a regular nonagon.
   Describe the figures:
      i) KLMNPQRST
     ii) IFC
     iii) ABHI

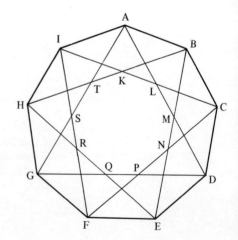

6. ABCDEFGHIJ is a regular decagon.
Describe the figures:
   i) ACEGI   ii) KLMNP
iii) ACNI   iv) CEGI
   v) AMNP

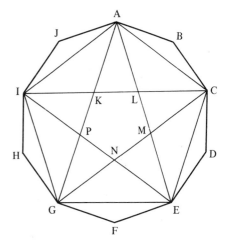

7. ABCDEFGHIJKL is a regular
12-sided polygon. Describe the
figures:
   i) UVWXYZ   ii) PQS
iii) PWRZ   iv) UVSQ

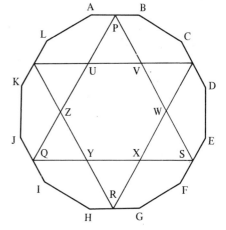

8. ABCDEFGHIJKL is a regular
12-sided polygon. Describe the
figures:
   i) WXYZ
   ii) MNPQRSTU

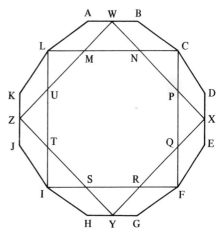

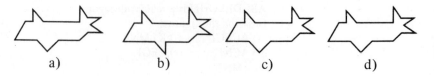

If you look at the above drawings carefully you should see that three of them, a), c) and d) are exactly the same.

Shapes that are alike in every possible way, sides, angles and area, are said to be *congruent*.

Example 1

Pick out the congruent shapes from the following:

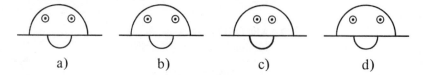

a), b) and d) are the congruent shapes.

Exercise 26

Pick out the congruent shapes from the following.

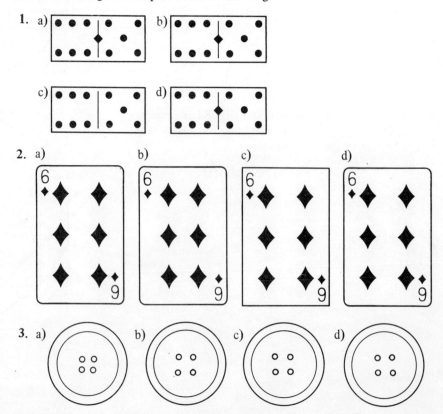

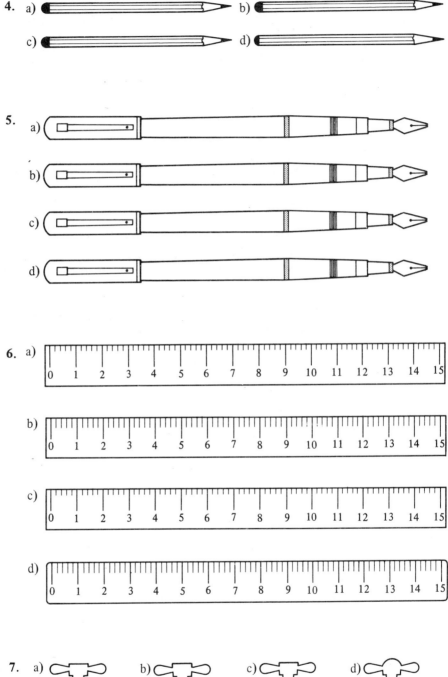

4. a) b)

c) d)

5. a)

b)

c)

d)

6. a)

b)

c)

d)

7. a) b) c) d)

8. a)

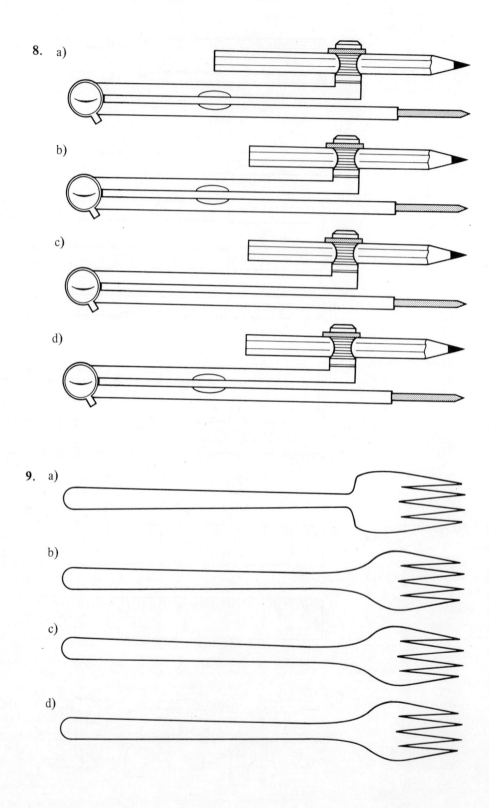

b)

c)

d)

9. a)

b)

c)

d)

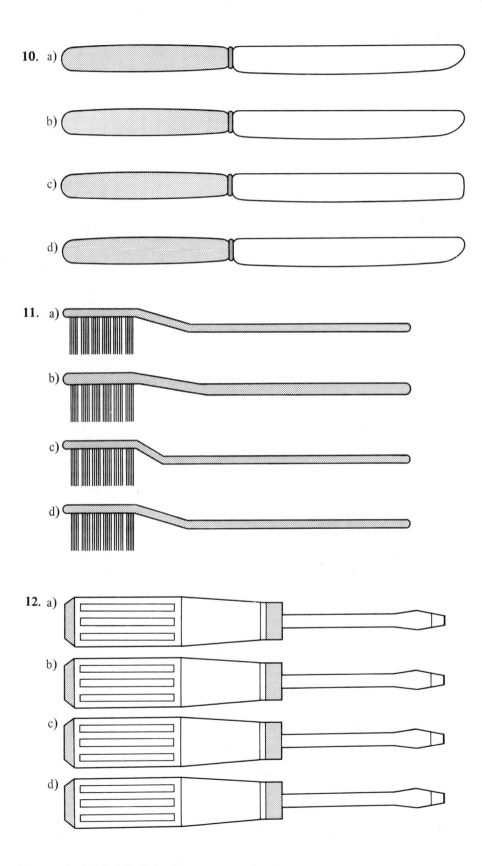

10. a)

b)

c)

d)

11. a)

b)

c)

d)

12. a)

b)

c)

d)

13. a)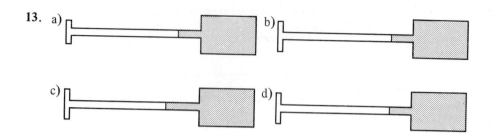

14. a)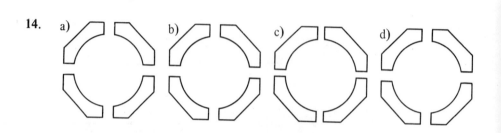

15. a)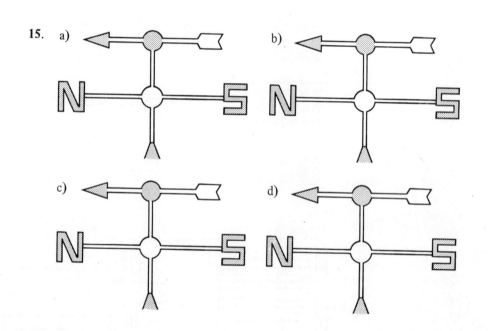

Example 2

Draw sketches to show how four obtuse-angled isosceles triangles, all of which are congruent, can be arranged to make:

a) one large obtuse-angled isosceles triangle,
b) a parallelogram in two different ways.

a)

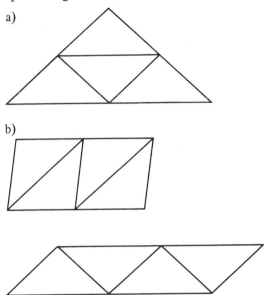

b)

Exercise 27

1. Draw sketches to show how four acute-angled isosceles triangles, all of which are congruent, can be arranged to make:
   a) one large acute-angled isosceles triangle,
   b) a parallelogram in two different ways.

2. Draw a sketch to show how four congruent equilateral triangles can be arranged to make one large equilateral triangle.

3. Draw sketches to show how four right-angled isosceles triangles, all of which are congruent, can be arranged to make:
   a) one large right-angled isosceles triangle,
   b) a rectangle.

4. Draw sketches to show how four congruent right-angled triangles can be arranged to make:
   a) one large right-angled triangle,
   b) a rectangle in two different ways,
   c) a parallelogram in two different ways,
   d) an isosceles trapezium in two different ways.

5. Draw a sketch to show how six congruent equilateral triangles can be arranged to make a regular hexagon.

6. Draw a sketch to show how three congruent rhombuses can be arranged to make a hexagon.

7. The illustration shows four congruent right-angled triangles. The lengths of the sides which meet at the right angle are in the ratio of 2:1. Draw a sketch to show how the four triangles could be arranged to make a square.

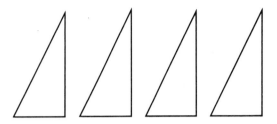

8. The illustration shows four right-angled isosceles triangles, all of which are congruent, and one square whose dimension is equal to the length of the longest side of any of the triangles. Draw a sketch to show how the five figures could be arranged to make a square.

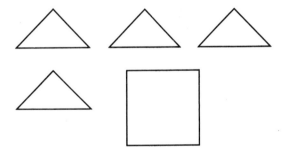

9. The illustration shows four congruent isosceles trapeziums and one square. The lengths of the parallel sides of the trapeziums are in the ratio of 3:1, and the dimension of the square is equal to the length of the shorter parallel side of any of the trapeziums. Draw a sketch to show how the five figures could be arranged to make a square.

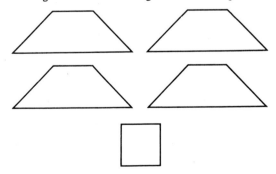

10. The illustration shows a kite whose longer pair of equal sides meet at an angle of 90°, and whose illustrated diagonal is equal in length to these two sides. Draw a sketch to show how four congruent kites of this kind could be arranged to make a regular octagon.

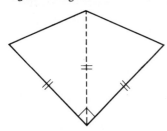

Example 3

Pick out and name the three pairs of congruent triangles from the kite ABCD.

The congruent triangles are:

a) ADM and ABM
b) ADC and ABC
c) DMC and BMC

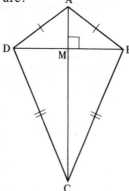

Exercise 28

1. Pick out and name the single pair of congruent triangles from the isosceles trapezium ABCD.

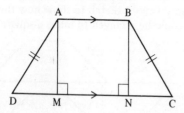

2. Pick out and name the single pair of congruent triangles from the isosceles triangle ABC.

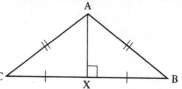

3. Pick out and name the single pair of congruent triangles from the kite ABCD.

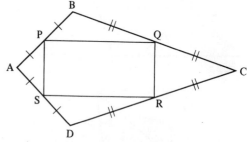

4. Pick out and name the two pairs of congruent triangles from the regular hexagon ABCDEF.

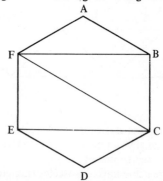

5. Pick out and name the two pairs of congruent triangles from the rhombus ABCD. (W, X, Y and Z are the mid-points of the sides.)

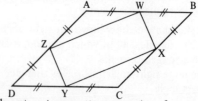

6. Pick out and name the two pairs of congruent triangles from the isosceles trapezium ABCD. (K, L, M and N are the mid-points of the sides.)

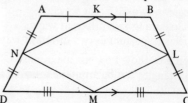

7. Pick out and name the two pairs of congruent triangles from the regular pentagon ABCDE. (M is the mid-point of CD.)

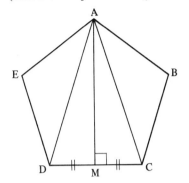

8. Pick out and name the three pairs of congruent triangles from the kite ABCD.

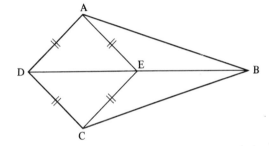

9. Pick out and name the three pairs of congruent triangles from the regular octagon ABCDEFGH.

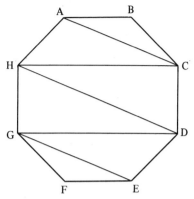

10. Pick out and name the three pairs of congruent triangles from the isosceles trapezium ABCD.

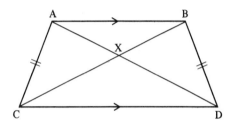

2.5 CONSTRUCTIONS

Remember that for true constructions only a pencil, a ruler and a pair of compasses are used.

Example 1

To drop a perpendicular from a given point onto a straight line.

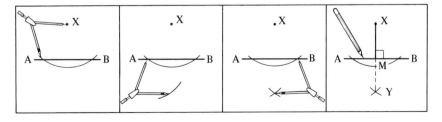

Follow each step carefully. X is the given point, AB is the straight line and XM is the required perpendicular.

Example 2

To construct a triangle given the lengths of the three sides.

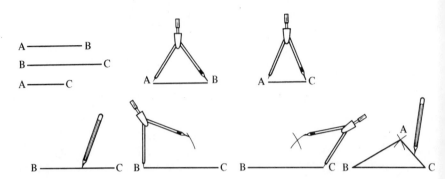

The lines AB, BC and AC are the given three sides and △ABC is the finished figure.

Exercise 29

Construct the triangle ABC for each of the following sets of given sides. Measure the three angles of the triangle for each case.

1. AB = 8 cm, BC = 11 cm and AC = 9·8 cm.
2. AB = 8 cm, BC = 7·1 cm and AC = 7·8 cm.
3. AB = 10 cm, BC = 13 cm and AC = 5·6 cm.
4. AB = 10 cm, BC = 8 cm and AC = 10 cm.
5. AB = 10 cm, BC = 15 cm and AC = 10 cm.
6. AB = 5 cm, BC = 9 cm and AC = 5 cm.
7. AB = 7 cm, BC = 8 cm and AC = 4 cm.
8. AB = 9 cm, BC = 10 cm and AC = 4 cm.

Construct the triangle ABC for each of the following sets of given sides. For each case drop a perpendicular from A down to BC and measure the length of this perpendicular

9. AB = 10 cm, BC = 13 cm and AC = 12·6 cm.
10. AB = 4 cm, BC = 8 cm and AC = 5 cm.
11. AB = 8 cm, BC = 11 cm and AC = 5·6 cm.
12. AB = 9 cm, BC = 9·9 cm and AC = 5 cm.
13. AB = 4 cm, BC = 7 cm and AC = 4 cm.
14. AB = 7 cm, BC = 10 cm and AC = 7 cm.
15. AB = BC = AC = 8 cm.

Example 3

To construct a parallelogram given two sides and the included angle.

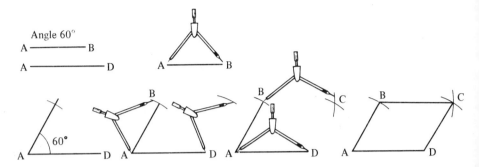

The lines AB and AD are the given sides and 60° is the included angle.

Draw the line AD and construct an angle of 60° at A. Follow the steps carefully and then ABCD is the required parallelogram.

Exercise 30

Construct the parallelogram ABCD for each case. Measure the lengths of the diagonals for each case also.

1. AB = 4 cm, AD = 8 cm and the included angle = 60°.
2. AB = 8 cm, AD = 11 cm and the included angle = 60°.
3. AB = AD = 8 cm and the included angle = 60°.
4. AB = 5·6 cm, AD = 13 cm and the included angle = 45°.
5. AB = 4 cm, AD = 8 cm and the included angle = 30°.
6. AB = 4 cm, AD = 7 cm and the included angle = 90°.
7. AB = 4 cm, AD = 9 cm and the included angle = 90°.
8. AB = AD = 5 cm and the included angle = 90°.

REVISION EXERCISE B

1. Look at the star pattern illustrated.
   a) Describe the figure ABCDEF.
   b) Find the sizes of the following angles:
      i) FÂB,   ii) PÂB and
      iii) the vertex angle AP̂B.
   c) What is the sum of the sizes of all the vertex angles in the pattern?

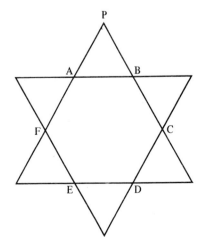

2. Look at the star pattern illustrated.

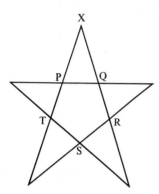

a) Describe the figure PQRST.

b) Find the sizes of the following angles:
   i) TP̂Q,   ii) XP̂Q
   iii) the vertex angle PX̂Q.

c) What is the sum of the sizes of all the vertex angles in the pattern?

3. The diagram illustrates the top of a fence stake. Find the size of angles a and b.

4. The head of the arrow below is an isosceles triangle and its two flights are parallelograms.

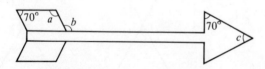

Find the size of the angles a, b and c.

5. The equilateral triangle illustrated is made from four smaller triangles of the same kind which are all congruent.

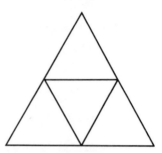

Draw a sketch which shows how the four triangles could be rearranged to make a parallelogram.

6. The rectangle illustrated is made from one isosceles triangle and two right-angled triangles which are congruent.

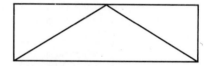

Draw sketches to show how the same three figures could be rearranged to make i) an isosceles trapezium, ii) a parallelogram, iii) a rhombus.

7. The square illustrated is made from a smaller square and four isosceles right-angled triangles which are congruent.

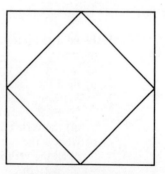

Draw sketches to show how the same five figures could be rearranged to make i) an isosceles trapezium, ii) a parallelogram, iii) one large isosceles right-angled triangle, iv) a rectangle.

A graph compares two quantities. You will discover that the points given by these quantities on a graph often form a straight line; for example,

distances on a map against real distances on land.

Example 1

The table below shows the real distance in kilometres and the map distance in centimetres between various towns.

Real distance (km)	0	5	7·5	12·5
Map distance (cm)	0	2	3	5

Using a scale of 1 cm to represent 2 km on the horizontal axis and a scale of 1 cm to represent 1 cm on the vertical axis, draw a suitable graph.

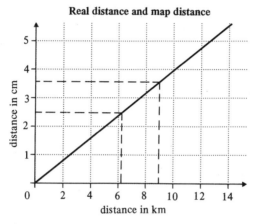

From your graph, estimate

a) the distance on the map of two towns which are 9 km apart
b) the real distance between two towns when the map distance is 2·5 cm

a) Map distance is 3·6 cm
b) Real distance is 6·3 km

Exercise 31

1. A flight of stairs reaches a height of 3 metres above the lower floor.
   The table on the next page shows the height of certain stairs above the floor.

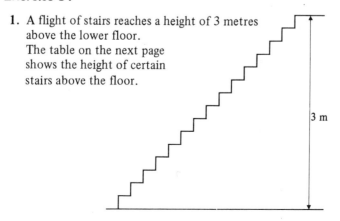

No. of stairs	2	4	5	10	13	15
Height above floor (cm)	40	80	100	200	260	300

Draw a graph of the figures in the table using a horizontal scale of 1 cm to 1 stair and a vertical scale of 1 cm to 20 cm.
a) Find from your graph the height above the floor of i) the third stair, ii) the seventh stair, iii) the ninth stair, iv) the eleventh stair.
b) Find from your graph which stair I am standing on if my feet are i) 120 cm, ii) 160 cm, iii) 240 cm, iv) 280 cm above the floor.

2. The length of a spring is 10 cm. The spring is stretched by hanging weights from its end. The new lengths are given in the table.

Weight (g)	0	10	15	30	45	60
Length (cm)	10	12	13	16	19	22

Draw a graph of this information using a horizontal scale of 1 cm to 5 g and a vertical scale of 1 cm to 1 cm.
a) Find from your graph the length of the spring supporting a weight of i) 5 g, ii) 25 g, iii) 40 g, iv) 55 g.
b) Find from your graph the weight required to stretch the spring to a length of i) 14 cm, ii) 17 cm, iii) 20 cm.

3. The table shows the number of sheets of writing paper in a pile of a given height.

No. of sheets	100	250	350	500
Height of pile (mm)	8	20	28	40

Draw a graph of this information using a horizontal scale of 1 cm to 50 sheets and a vertical scale of 1 cm to 2 mm.
a) What is the height of a pile containing i) 50 sheets, ii) 150 sheets, iii) 400 sheets?
b) Find the number of sheets of paper in a pile of height i) 16 mm, ii) 24 mm, iii) 36 mm.

4. The table gives the weight of each pile of writing paper listed in question 3.

No. of sheets	100	250	350	500
Weight of pile (g)	400	1000	1400	2000

Display this information on a graph using a horizontal scale of 1 cm to 50 sheets and a vertical scale of 1 cm to 100 g.
a) Use your graph to find the weight of a pile of i) 50 sheets, ii) 200 sheets, iii) 300 sheets.
b) What is the number of sheets in a pile weighing i) 600 g, ii) 1600 g, iii) 1800 g?

5. The table shows the number of lumps of sugar of equal size contained in three different weights of packet.

Weight of packet (g)	200	320	400	600
No. of lumps	60	96	120	180

Draw a graph to illustrate this information using a horizontal scale of 1 cm to 50 g and a vertical scale of 1 cm to 10 sugar lumps.
a) How many sugar lumps could be contained in a packet weighing i) 500 g, ii) 560 g?
b) Find the weight of a packet containing 144 lumps of sugar.

6. A girl produced this table of money equivalents for her Belgian pen friend.

British money	£1	£3	£4·50	£7	£8
Belgian francs	60	180	270	420	480

Plot a graph of this information using a horizontal scale of 2 cm to £1 and a vertical scale of 2 cm to 100 Belgian francs.
a) From your graph find the value in Belgian francs of i) 50p, ii) £2, iii) £3·50, iv) £7·50
b) What is the value in British money of i) 150 Belgian francs, ii) 240 Belgian francs, iii) 390 Belgian francs?

7. The cost of a certain kind of curtain track is shown in the table.

Length of window (cm)	80	100	140	200	250
Cost of curtain track	48p	60p	84p	£1·20	£1·50

Show this information on a graph using a horizontal scale of 1 cm to 10 cm and a vertical scale of 1 cm to 10p.
What is the cost of curtain track for a window of length i) 150 cm, ii) 180 cm, iii) 240 cm?

8. Six children are standing together in the sunshine. For some of the children the heights and shadow lengths are given in the table below.

Name	Wendy	David	Carol	Paul
Height (cm)	100	120	132	160
Shadow length (cm)	150	180	198	240

Using a scale of 1 cm to 10 cm on both axes, plot a graph of the above figures. (Use the horizontal axis for the heights.)

Find from your graph:
 i) the length of Keith's shadow if he is 140 cm tall
 ii) the length of Elizabeth's shadow if she is 108 cm tall.

9. Eight children have their photographs taken together. For some of the children, their real heights and their heights on the snapshot are given in the table below.

Name	Anne	Robert	William	Peter
Real height (cm)	110	120	140	180
Height on snapshot (mm)	55	60	70	90

Using a scale of 1 cm to 10 cm on the horizontal axis and a scale of 1 cm to 5 mm on the vertical axis, draw a graph of the above figures.

Find from your graph:
a) the height on the snapshot of i) Mary, who is 130 cm tall and ii) Jane, who is 160 cm tall.
b) the real height of i) Julie, who is 75 mm tall on the snapshot and ii) John, who is 85 mm tall on the snapshot.

10. The girls in class 4A have either auburn, blonde or dark hair. Details are given in the table below.

Colour of hair	Auburn	Blonde	Dark
Number of girls	2	6	12
Percentage of girls	10%	30%	60%

Using a scale of 1 cm to 1 girl on the horizontal axis and a scale of 1 cm to 5% on the vertical axis draw a graph of the above figures.

Find the answers to the following from your graph:
 i) If 8 girls are hockey players what percentage of the class are hockey players?
 ii) If 11 girls are netball players what percentage of the class are netball players?
 iii) If 14 girls have blue eyes what percentage of the class have blue eyes?
 iv) One day 15% of the girls arrive late. How many girls arrive late?
 v) 25% of the girls cycle to school. What number of girls cycle to school?
 vi) On a certain day 80% of the girls are present. What number of girls are present?

3.2 INEQUALITIES

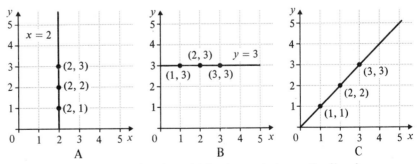

In graph A, all the ordered pairs which give points on the line have an x-value of 2; the line is the graph of $x = 2$.

In graph B, all the ordered pairs which give points on the line have a y-value of 3; the line is the graph of $y = 3$.

In graph C, all the ordered pairs which give points on the line have the x-value equal to the y-value; the line is the graph of $y = x$.

Example 1

Give the equation
of the line for
the graphs a) and
b).

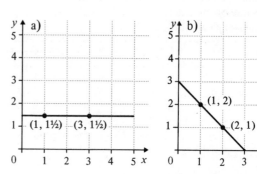

a) As all the points on the line have a y-value of $1\frac{1}{2}$, the graph is $y = 1\frac{1}{2}$.
b) As all the points on the line are such that the x-value added to the
   y-value equals 3, the graph is $x + y = 3$.

Exercise 32

Give the equation of the line for each of the following graphs:

1.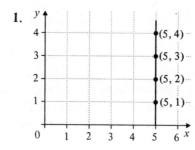

2.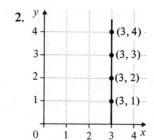

3.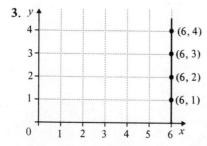

4.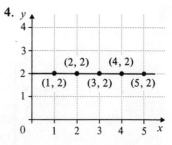

5.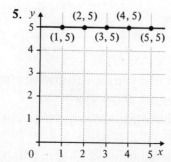

6.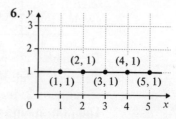

7.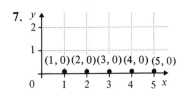

8.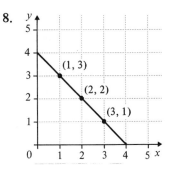

9.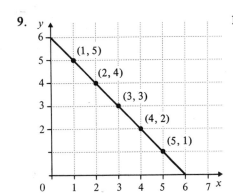

10.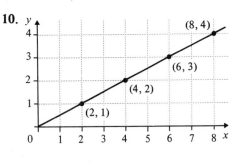

Draw the graphs of the following equations:

11. $x = 4$	**12.** $x = 1$	**13.** $x = 7$	**14.** $x = 0$
15. $y = 4$	**16.** $y = 6$	**17.** $y = 3$	**18.** $x + y = 5$
19. $x + y = 2$	**20.** $y = 3x$		

On the graph illustrated, any ordered pair that gives the position of a point in the shaded region A will have a y-value that is less than 3.

The shaded area A is therefore the region $y < 3$.

The non-shaded area B is the region $y > 3$.

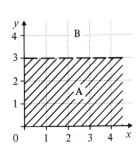

In this graph the shaded area
B includes the line $x = 4$;
B is the region $x \geqslant 4$.

The non-shaded area A is the
region $x \leqslant 4$.

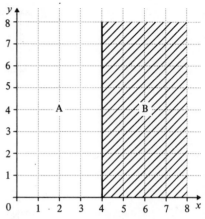

When drawing or describing regions on a graph remember the following
two points:

i) A broken line indicates that no point in the region lies on the line.
ii) An unbroken line indicates that all points on the line are included in
the region.

Example 2

Describe the following shaded regions.

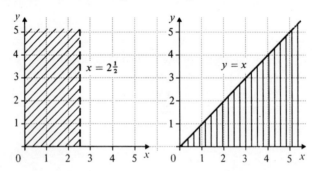

a) The region is $x < 2\frac{1}{2}$.   b) The region is $y \leqslant x$.

Example 3

Illustrate the following regions:

a) $y \leqslant 2$ b) $x + y > 4$

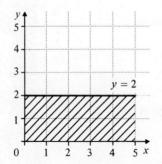
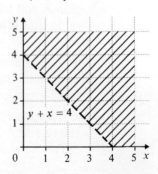

Exercise 33

Describe the following shaded regions:

1.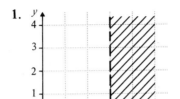

2.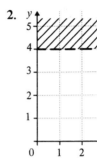

3.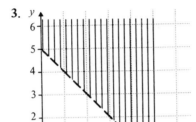

4.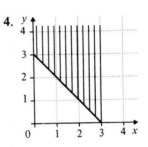

5.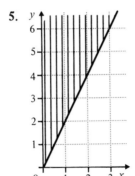

6.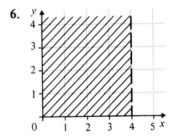

7.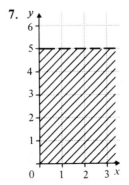

8.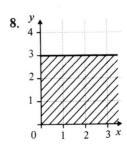

9.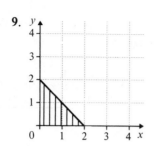

10.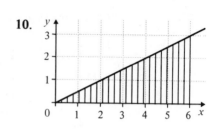

Illustrate the following regions:

11. $x > 5$ **12.** $y > 3$ **13.** $y \geqslant 6$ **14.** $x + y \geqslant 6$ **15.** $y \geqslant 3x$

16. $x < 2$ **17.** $y < 7$ **18.** $x + y < 4$ **19.** $x \leqslant 3$ **20.** $y \leqslant 5$

REVISION EXERCISE C

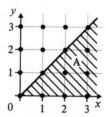   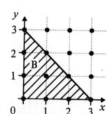

1. a) Make a list of the coordinates of the 16 points on the grid of the two graphs shown above.
   b) State whether each point is in region A, in region B, in both regions, or in neither region.
   c) Draw a large Venn diagram similar to that on the right in which
      $\mathscr{E} = \{\text{all the 16 points}\}$
      $A = \{\text{points in region A}\}$
      $B = \{\text{points in region B}\}$
   d) Enter the coordinates of all 16 points in the correct place on the Venn diagram.

2. Draw a similar Venn diagram to question **1**, entering the coordinates of all 16 points for the graphs below for regions P and Q.

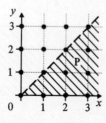   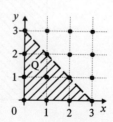

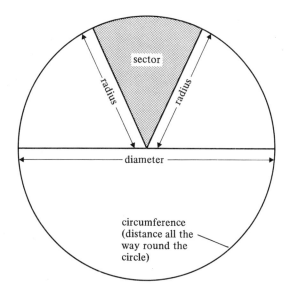

The diagram shows the names of the parts of a circle.

Exercise 34

For each of the circles numbered **1** to **5** below, measure the diameter.

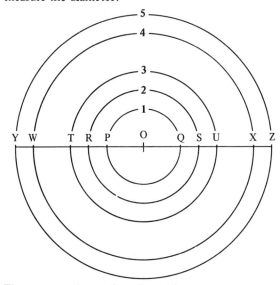

Then copy and complete this table.

Circle	diameter D	circumference C	$C \div D$
1	PQ = cm	6·28 cm	. . .
2	RS = cm	9·42 cm	. . .
3	TU = cm	12·56 cm	. . .
4	WX = cm	18·84 cm	. . .
5	YZ = 7 cm	22·0 cm	$\frac{22}{7} \approx 3·14$

If you have been accurate in calculating the value $C \div D$ in Exercise 34, you will find that all the results equal 3·14.

The ratio $\dfrac{C}{D}$ is the same for all circles; it is represented by the Greek letter π (pi).

$$\pi = \frac{C}{D} \approx 3·14 \approx \frac{22}{7}$$

The symbol $\approx$ means 'approximately'.

Because $\dfrac{C}{D} = \pi$

then $C = \pi D = 2\pi r$

where r is the radius of the circle.

Example 1

Find the circumference of the following circles.

a) diameter = 6 cm (take $\pi = 3·14$)

b) radius   = 7 cm (take $\pi = \frac{22}{7}$)

a) circumference = πD

$$= 3·14 \times 6 = 18·84 \text{ cm}$$

b) circumference = πD

$$= 2\pi r = 2 \times \tfrac{22}{7} \times 7$$

$$= \frac{2}{1} \times \frac{22}{\cancel{7}} \times \frac{\cancel{7}^{1}}{1} = 44 \text{ cm}$$

Exercise 35

Find the circumference of each of the following circles (take $\pi = \frac{22}{7}$)

1. diameter = 21 cm   2. diameter = 35 cm
3. diameter = 49 cm   4. diameter = 63 cm
5. diameter = 77 mm   6. diameter = 140 mm
7. radius = 35 cm   8. radius = 14 cm
9. radius = 21 cm   10. radius = 28 cm
11. radius = 42 mm   12. radius = 105 mm

Find the circumference of each of the following circles (take $\pi = 3·14$)

13. diameter = 9 cm   14. diameter = 20 mm
15. diameter = 12 mm   16. radius = 4 cm
17. radius = $3\frac{1}{2}$ cm   18. radius = 2·5 cm

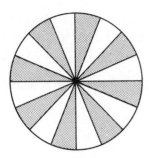

If a circle is divided into 16 equal sectors, the sectors will almost fit into a parallelogram whose area is the same as that of the circle.

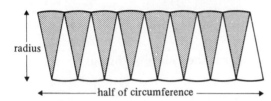

radius

half of circumference

area of parallelogram

= base × height

= (half of circumference) × radius

$= \dfrac{2\pi r}{2} \times r = \pi r \times r = \pi r^2$

So the area of a circle $= \pi r^2$.

Example 2

Find the area of the following circles:

a) radius = 10 cm (take $\pi = 3\cdot142$)

b) diameter = 14 m (take $\pi \; \frac{22}{7}$)

a) area $= \pi r^2 = 3\cdot142 \times 10 \times 10 = 31\cdot42 \times 10$
$$= 314\cdot2 \text{ cm}^2.$$

b) radius $= \frac{1}{2} \times$ diameter $= \frac{1}{2} \times 14 = 7$ m

$$\text{area} \;= \pi r^2 = \frac{22}{7} \times \frac{7}{1} \times \frac{7}{1} = \frac{22}{7} \times \frac{7}{1} \times \frac{7}{1}$$

$$= 154 \text{ m}^2.$$

Exercise 36

Find the area of the following circles (take $\pi = 3\cdot14$).

1. radius = 2 cm   2. radius = 4 cm
3. diameter = 6 cm   4. diameter = 10 cm
5. radius = 0·1 m

Find the area of the following circles (take $\pi = 3\cdot142$).

6. radius = 0·2 m   7. radius = 0·5 m
8. diameter = 0·6 m   9. diameter = 0·8 m
10. diameter = 20 mm

Find the area of the following circles (take $\pi = 3\cdot1$).

11. radius = 30 mm   12. radius = 20 mm
13. radius = 90 mm   14. diameter = 120 mm

Find the area of the following circles (take $\pi = \frac{22}{7}$).

15. radius = 70 mm   16. radius = $3\frac{1}{2}$ cm
17. radius = 14 cm   18. diameter = 42 cm
19. diameter = 1·4 m   20. radius = $1\frac{2}{5}$ m

Example 3

The diameter of a cotton reel is 2·1 cm. If the cotton is wound round the reel 1500 times, what is the length of the thread? (take $\pi = \frac{22}{7}$)

one turn of the thread = circumference of reel

$$= \frac{22}{7} \times 2\cdot1 = \frac{22}{7} \times \frac{21}{10} = \frac{66}{10} = 6\cdot6 \text{ cm}$$

therefore, total length of thread

$= 6\cdot6 \times 1500$ cm

$= 9900$ cm

$= 99$ m.

Exercise 37

1. The diameter of a reel of wire is 14 cm. If the wire is wound round the reel 50 times, find the length of the wire, a) in centimetres, b) in metres. (Take $\pi = \frac{22}{7}$).
2. Peter's bicycle has a front wheel of diameter 50 cm. Find the distance that he has cycled after the front wheel has turned round 500 times. Give your answer in metres (take $\pi = 3\cdot14$).
3. William has a marble of diameter 1·4 cm. He rolls it towards another marble which is 66 cm away. How many revolutions will his marble make before hitting the second one? (Take $\pi = \frac{22}{7}$).

4. Gillian has a hoop of diameter 1·05 m. How many revolutions will it make shile she rolls it along her garden path which is 16·5 m in length? (Take $\pi = \frac{22}{7}$).

5. A push button switch which operates a door bell has a radius of 5 mm. Find its surface area. (Take $\pi = 3·14$).

6. A dart board has a radius of 28 cm. Find its surface area. (Take $\pi = \frac{22}{7}$).

4.2 VOLUME

A *prism* is any solid which has a uniform cross section and plane sides.

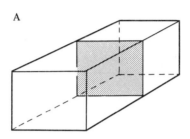
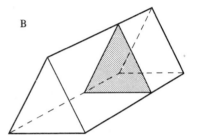

All prisms take their name from this cross section. Thus B is a *triangular* prism.

A prism having a rectangular cross section is a *cuboid*. Thus A is a cuboid. A *cube* has all its twelve edges equal in length.

Exercise 38

Name the following prisms.

 1.
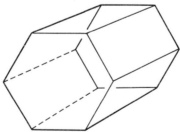

 2.
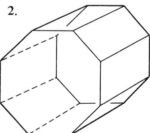

3.
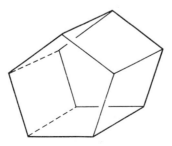

4.
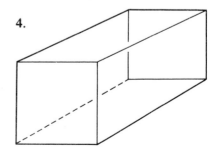

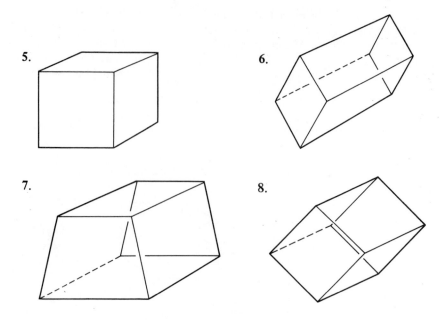

5.

6.

7.

8.

A *cylinder* is a solid of uniform circular cross section.

The volume V of any solid of uniform cross section is

$$V = A \times l$$

where A is the area of the cross section and l is the length of the solid.

Example 1

Find the volume of each of the following solids (take $\pi = 3{\cdot}14$ when required).

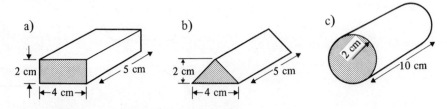

a)

b)

c)

a) Area of cross section $= 4 \times 2 = 8$ cm²
      length of solid $= 5$ cm
  ∴ Volume of solid $= 8 \times 5 = 40$ cm³

b) Area of cross section $= \frac{1}{2} \times 4 \times 2 = 4$ cm²
      length of solid $= 5$ cm
  ∴ Volume of solid $= 4 \times 5 = 20$ cm³

c) Area of cross section $= \pi \times 2 \times 2 = 3{\cdot}14 \times 2 \times 2 = 12{\cdot}56$ cm²
      length of solid $= 10$ cm
  ∴ Volume of solid $= 12{\cdot}56 \times 10 = 125{\cdot}6$ cm³

Exercise 39

In questions **1** to **7**, find the volume of each cuboid.

1.

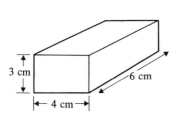

width = 4 cm; height = 3 cm;
length = 6 cm

2.

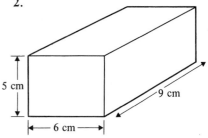

width = 6 cm; height = 5 cm;
length = 9 cm

3. width = 3 cm; height = 5 cm;
length = 6 cm

4. width = 4 cm; height = 4 cm;
length = 5 cm

5. width = 10 mm; height = 5 mm;
length = 20 mm

6. width = 5 mm; height = 8 mm;
length = 12 mm

7. width = 2 m; height = 1·5 m; length = 4 m

In questions **8** to **14**, find the volume of each triangular prism.

8.

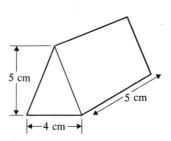

width = 4 cm; height = 5 cm;
length = 5 cm

9.

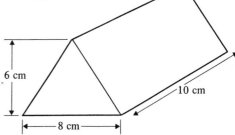

width = 8 cm; height = 6 cm;
length = 10 cm

10. width = 6 cm; height = 5 cm;
length = 7 cm

11. width = 4 cm; height = 6 cm;
length = 8 cm

12. width = 3 cm; height = 8 cm;
length = 12 cm

13. width = 10 mm; height = 6 mm;
length = 12 mm

14. width = 8 mm; height = 4 mm;
length = 15 mm

In questions **15** to **20**, find the volume of each cylinder.

15.

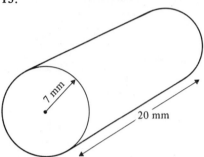

16.

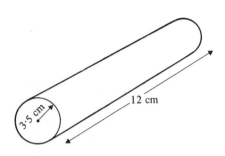

radius = 7 mm; length = 20 mm, take $\pi = \frac{22}{7}$

radius = 3·5 cm; length = 12 cm; take $\pi = \frac{22}{7}$

17. radius = 5 cm; length = 8 cm; take $\pi = 3·14$

18. radius = 4 cm; length = 5 cm; take $\pi = 3·14$

19. radius = 3 cm; length = 7 cm; take $\pi = \frac{22}{7}$

20. radius = 10 mm; length = 35 mm; take $\pi = \frac{22}{7}$

Example 2

The solid illustrated has a uniform cross section, and the dimensions shown. Find its volume.

area of cross section
$$= (3 \times 1) + (1 \times 2) + (2 \times 1)$$
$$= 3 + 2 + 2 = 7 \text{ cm}^2$$

length = 5 cm

$\therefore$ volume of solid
$$= 7 \times 5 = 35 \text{ cm}^2$$

Exercise 40

Each of the solids illustrated has a uniform cross section. Find the volume of each solid from the dimensions given.

1.

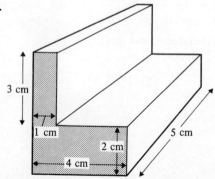

2.

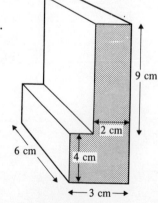

3.

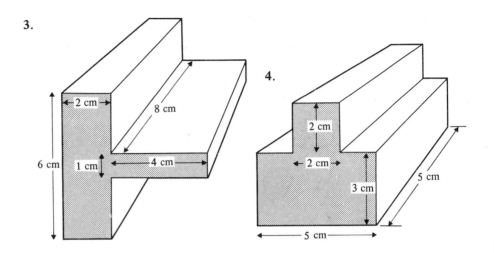

4.

5.

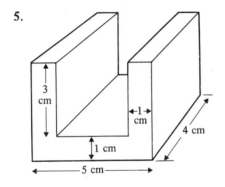

6.

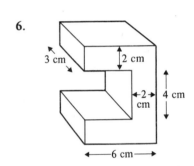

7.

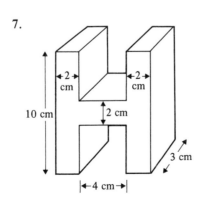

8.

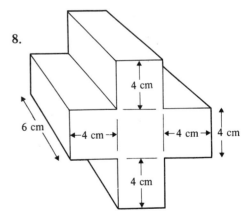

Example 3

A beef stock cube has sides of length 2 cm.
How many stock cubes would fill a box
measuring 6 cm × 4 cm × 4 cm?

Volume of box = 6 × 4 × 4 = 96 cm³

Volume of stock cube = 8 cm³

∴ number of cubes in the box = 96 ÷ 8 = 12

Exercise 41

1. A wooden block measures 20 cm × 12 cm × 8 cm.
   It is sawn up into toy bricks each measuring
   4 cm × 4 cm × 4 cm. How many toy bricks can
   be made from the wooden block?
2. A packet of chocolate biscuits measures
   24 cm × 5 cm × 4 cm. How many chocolate
   biscuits can be contained in the full packet if
   each measures 5 cm × 2 cm × 2 cm?
3. A wholesale pack of ice cream brickettes measures
   30 cm × 12 cm × 12 cm. If each brickette
   measures 10 cm × 6 cm × 2 cm, how many are
   contained in a full pack?
4. The art teacher keeps pencil rubbers in a box
   measuring 9 cm × 4 cm × 2 cm. How many
   rubbers can be placed in the box if each measures
   3 cm × 2 cm × 5 mm?
5. A solid brickwork pillar forms a gate post 1 m high
   having a cross section measuring 60 cm by 60 cm.
   It is built of bricks each measuring
   30 cm × 15 cm × 10 cm. How many bricks were
   used to build the pillar?
6. A packet of sugar lumps has the dimensions
   60 mm × 50 mm × 60 mm. If each lump of sugar
   measures 12 mm × 12 mm × 10 mm, how many
   lumps are there in a full packet?

Example 4

Find the capacity in litres of each of the tanks
shown. (1 m³ = 1000 litres; take π = 3·14)

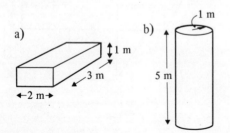

a) area of cross section = 2 × 1 = 2m²
   length of tank = 3 m
   ∴ volume = 2 × 3 = 6 m³
   and capacity = 6 × 1000
                = 6000 litres

b) area of cross section = π × 1 × 1 = 3·14 cm²
   height of tank = 5 m
   ∴ volume = 3·14 × 5 = 15·7 m³
   and capacity = 15·7 × 1000
                = 15 700 litres

Exercise 42

Find the capacity in litres of each tank.
(1 m³ = 1000 litres; 1000 cm³ = 1 litre)

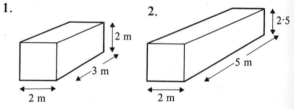

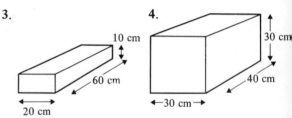

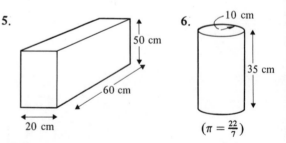

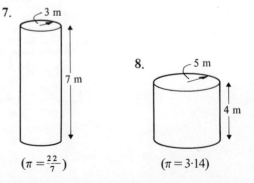

9. A house is heated by an oil-fired boiler. The supply tank has a rectangular base measuring 120 cm by 70 cm.
   a) If the depth of oil in the tank is 100 cm, how many litres of oil does the tank contain?
   b) The burner consumes 12 litres of oil per day. For how many weeks will this oil supply last?

10. In a café cold milk is served from a machine. The milk is contained in a plastic tank measuring 30 cm by 30 cm by 30 cm.
   a) How many litres of milk does the tank contain when full?
   b) The milk served in plastic cups each containing $\frac{1}{5}$ litre. How many cups can be served from the full tank?

11. An inflatable paddling pool has a radius of 70 cm.
   a) How many litres of water does the pool contain if the depth of water is 20 cm? (Take $\pi = \frac{22}{7}$).
   b) The pool is filled to this depth using a bucket of capacity 28 litres. How many buckets full of water are required?

12. A cylindrical coffee urn has a radius of 20 cm.
   a) If the depth of coffee in the urn is 35 cm, how many litres does it contain? (Take $\pi = \frac{22}{7}$).
   b) How many cups of coffee, each of capacity $\frac{11}{50}$ of a litre, can be served?

REVISION EXERCISE D

For each question, find which of the three solids has a different volume from the other two. Where necessary, assume $\pi = \frac{22}{7}$.

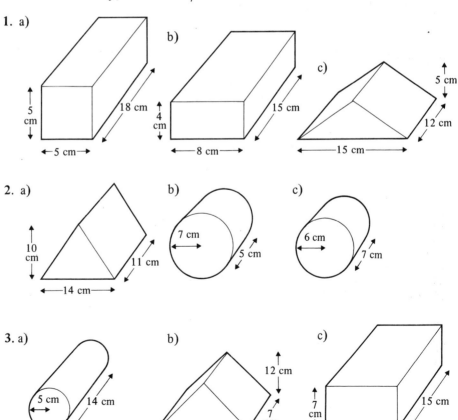

$2 \times 3 = 3 \times 2$

In the same way,

$$a \times b = b \times a$$
$$ab = ba$$

So $ab + ba = 2ab$

Example 1

Simplify the following by collecting like terms.

a) $3a - 2b - 5a + 5b$
b) $2ab + 3ba - 4ab$

a) $3a - 2b - 5a + 5b$

   $= 3a - 5a - 2b + 5b$

   $= -2a + 3b$

   $= 3b - 2a$

b) $2ab + 3ba - 4ab$

   $= 2ab + 3ab - 4ab$

   $= 5ab - 4ab$

   $= ab$

Exercise 43

Simplify the following by collecting like terms.

1. $4a + 3a + 2a$	**2.** $6b + 4b + b$
3. $9c + 3c - 2c$	**4.** $2d + 5d - 4d$
5. $5m + 3m - 4m$	**6.** $7n + 2n - 8n$
7. $9p - 4p - 2p$	**8.** $12q - 6q - 3q$
9. $10r - 3r - r$	**10.** $11s - 6s - 4s$

11. $3x + 7y + 2x$	**12.** $8u + 2v + u$
13. $6a + 5b - 2a$	**14.** $7c + 3d - 5c$
15. $9m + 4n - m$	**16.** $5z + 7z^2 - 3z$
17. $10t + 8t^2 - 5t$	**18.** $3a + 2b + 6a + 5b$
19. $5c + 3d + 7c + 4d$	**20.** $2m + 7n + 9m + n$

21. $5p + 8q + 2p - 3q$	**22.** $7u + 5v + u - 2v$
23. $9x + 6y + 3x - 5y$	**24.** $8a + 9b - 2a - 4b$
25. $12c + 10d - 9c - 3d$	**26.** $9z^2 + 8z - 7z^2 - 3z$
27. $11t^2 + 10t - t^2 - 9t$	**28.** $5a + 4b - 2a - 6b$
29. $8c + 5d - 3c - 9d$	**30.** $10m + 3n - 8m - 6n$

31. $12z^2 + 4z - 2z^2 - 9z$	**32.** $8t^2 + 6t - t^2 - 10t$
33. $9p + q - 6p - 3q$	**34.** $11r + 5s - 7r - 6s$
35. $6u + 10v - 5u - 11v$	**36.** $3a + 9b - 5a - 4b$
37. $5c + 10d - 9c - 6d$	**38.** $4x + 12y - 7x - 8y$
39. $u + 11v - 3u - 6v$	**40.** $z^2 + 12z - 5z^2 - 9z$

41. $2t^2 + 5t - 3t^2 - t$	**42.** $6m + 2n - 7m - n$
43. $5p - 4q - 2p - 3q$	**44.** $8x - 5y - 3x - 3y$

45. $10a - 8b - 5a - 4b$	**46.** $12c - 7d - c - 3d$
47. $11m - 8n - 9m - n$	**48.** $2p - 9q - p - q$
49. $5ab + 4ba - 2ab$	**50.** $8cd + 2dc - 5cd$

51. $7mn + 5nm - 9mn$	**52.** $6rs + 5sr - 10rs$
53. $9xy - 3yx - 4xy$	**54.** $12uv - 5vu - 2uv$
55. $10mn - nm - 4mn$	**56.** $9xy - 6yx + 4xy$
57. $12pq - 8qp + 3pq$	**58.** $10uv - 5vu + uv$
59. $4ab - 7ba + 5ab$	**60.** $4cd - 5dc + cd$

$2a = a + a$

In the same way,

$$2(a + b) = (a + b) + (a + b) = a + b + a + b$$
$$= a + a + b + b$$
$$= 2a + 2b$$

Also,

$$3(x - y) = x - y + x - y + x - y$$
$$= x + x + x - y - y - y$$
$$= 3x - 3y$$

Each term inside the bracket has been multiplied by the number outside the bracket.

Example 2

Remove the brackets to simplify the following.

a) $6(x + 2)$ b) $-3(x + 3)$
c) $-2(x - y)$ d) $3(2x + 3y)$

a) $6(x + 2) = 6x + 12$

b) $-3(x + 3) = -3x - 9$
   because $-3 \times 3 = -9$

c) $-2(x - y) = -2x + 2y$
   because $-2 \times -1y = +2y$

d) $3(2x + 3y) = 6x + 9y$

Exercise 44

Remove the brackets to simplify the following.

1. $4(x + 2)$	**2.** $5(y + 3)$
3. $3(z + 4)$	**4.** $6(a + b)$
5. $2(p - 3)$	**6.** $4(q - 2)$
7. $3(r - 1)$	**8.** $5(c - d)$
9. $-3(a - 4)$	**10.** $-5(b - 2)$
11. $-4(c - 3)$	**12.** $-2(u - v)$

13. $-3(m + 2)$

14. $-4(n + 5)$

15. $-6(p + q)$

16. $2(3x + 2y)$

17. $4(2m + 5n)$

18. $5(3p + q)$

19. $3(u + 4v)$

20. $4(3a - 4b)$

21. $3(5c - 2d)$

22. $6(2m - n)$

23. $5(x - 5y)$

24. $-3(2p - 3q)$

25. $-4(5r - 4s)$

26. $-8(3u - v)$

27. $-2(a - 8b)$

28. $-5(6x + 5y)$

29. $-3(3m + n)$

30. $-7(c + 5d)$

b) $3(a + b) - 2(b - a)$

$= 3a + 3b - 2b + 2a$

$= 5a + b$

Exercise 45

For each question remove the brackets, then simplify by collecting like terms.

1. $3(x + y) + 2x$ 2. $2(u + v) + 4u$
3. $4(a + b) + a$ 4. $5(c + d) - 3c$
5. $6(m + n) - 2m$ 6. $4(p + q) + 3q$
7. $2(x + y) + 5y$ 8. $6(a + b) - 2b$
9. $8(c + d) - 6d$ 10. $5(m + n) - 4n$

11. $2(a + b) + 3(a + b)$ 12. $4(m + n) + 2(m - n)$
13. $6(p + q) + 5(p - q)$ 14. $4(u + v) + 6(u - v)$
15. $5(b + c) + 8(b - c)$ 16. $4(x - y) + 7(x + y)$

17. $3(a - b) + 4(a + b)$ 18. $5(c - d) + 2(c + d)$
19. $4(y - z) + 6(y - z)$ 20. $5(m - n) + 3(n - m)$

21. $7(p - q) + 2(q - p)$ 22. $5(x + y) - 2(x + y)$
23. $7(c - d) - 5(c + d)$ 24. $6(m - n) - 3(m + n)$
25. $4(p - q) - (p + q)$ 26. $5(u + v) - 3(u - v)$
27. $6(x + y) - 4(x - y)$ 28. $4(a + b) - 3(a - b)$
29. $10(m - n) - 2(m - n)$ 30. $5(p - q) - 4(p - q)$

Example 3

For the following, remove the brackets, then simplify by collecting like terms.

a) $4(x + y) - 3x$ b) $3(a + b) - 2(b - a)$

a) $4(x + y) - 3x$

$= 4x + 4y - 3x$

$= 4x - 3x + 4y$

$= x + 4y$

5.2 EQUATIONS

$3x + 5 = 14$

A relationship like this is called a simple linear equation.

Finding the value of x (which makes both sides of this equation equal) is called *solving* the equation.

For this equation, $x = 3$.

Both sides of an equation must always be equal. So, if one side is changed, then the other side of the equation must also be changed in the same way.

If $3x = 9$

then $x = 3$,

and this result is obtained by dividing both sides by 3.

If $4a = 3$

then $a = \frac{3}{4}$;

both sides are divided by 4.

Example 1

Solve the following equations.

a) $4x = 20$ b) $3b = -9$
c) $-2a = 10$ d) $-2a = -12$

a) $4x = 20$

Divide both sides by 4.

$$\frac{4x}{4} = \frac{20}{4}$$

$\Rightarrow$ $x = 5$

b) $3b = -9$

Divide both sides by 3.

$$\frac{3b}{3} = \frac{-9}{3}$$

$\Rightarrow$ $b = -3$

c)
$$-2a = 10$$
Divide both sides by -2.
$$\frac{-2a}{-2} = \frac{10}{-2}$$
$$\Rightarrow \quad a = -5$$

d)
$$-2a = -12$$
Divide both sides by -2.
$$\frac{-2a}{-2} = \frac{-12}{-2}$$
$$\Rightarrow \quad a = 6$$

Exercise 46

Solve the following equations.

1. $3x = 12$
2. $5x = 30$
3. $4x = 28$
4. $6y = 48$
5. $2y = 30$
6. $3z = 48$
7. $5a = 90$
8. $4b = 64$
9. $6c = 84$
10. $7d = 105$
11. $3x = -54$
12. $5x = -65$
13. $4y = -64$
14. $8z = -104$
15. $7t = -112$
16. $9a = -126$
17. $6b = -108$
18. $5c = -120$
19. $6m = -150$
20. $8n = -160$
21. $-4x = 68$
22. $-6x = 96$
23. $-5y = 95$
24. $-3y = 87$
25. $-7z = 98$
26. $-8t = 120$
27. $-6a = 102$
28. $-9b = 135$
29. $-7c = 133$
30. $-6d = 132$
31. $-5x = -75$
32. $-2x = -36$
33. $-3y = -72$
34. $-4y = -84$
35. $-7z = -119$
36. $-4a = -100$
37. $-8b = -144$
38. $-9c = -153$
39. $-6u = -150$
40. $-7v = -182$

If $x + 5 = 23$
then $\quad x = 18$

Here 5 has been subtracted from both sides of the equation.

If $x - 4 = 14$
then $\quad x = 18$

Here 4 has been added to both sides of the equation.

If $4a + 10 = 22$
then $\quad 4a = 12$
$$\Rightarrow \quad a = 3$$

Here 10 has been subtracted from both sides; then both sides have been divided by 4.

Example 2

Solve the following equations.

a) $x + 6 = 9$ 　　b) $3x + 5 = 11$
c) $4a - 10 = 22$

a)
$$x + 6 = 9$$
$$\Rightarrow \quad x = 3$$

Here 6 is subtracted from both sides.

b) $\quad 3x + 5 = 11$
$\Rightarrow \quad 3x = 6$ (subtract 5 from both sides)
$\Rightarrow \quad x = 2$ (divide both sides by 3)

c) $\quad 4a - 10 = 22$
$\Rightarrow \quad 4a = 32$ (add 10 to both sides)
$\Rightarrow \quad a = 8$ (divide both sides by 4)

Exercise 47

Solve the following equations.

1. $x + 5 = 7$
2. $x + 3 = 9$
3. $y + 4 = 8$
4. $y + 6 = 7$
5. $z + 2 = 10$
6. $z + 8 = 12$
7. $t + 5 = 11$
8. $t + 7 = 19$
9. $a + 9 = 16$
10. $b + 6 = 15$
11. $x - 3 = 4$
12. $x - 2 = 6$
13. $y - 4 = 5$
14. $y - 1 = 8$
15. $z - 5 = 3$
16. $z - 9 = 1$
17. $a - 8 = 4$
18. $a - 6 = 8$
19. $b - 8 = 10$
20. $c - 7 = 13$
21. $3x + 4 = 16$
22. $5x + 2 = 17$
23. $4y + 3 = 19$
24. $2y + 5 = 15$
25. $8z + 9 = 25$
26. $6a + 7 = 25$
27. $7b + 8 = 36$
28. $5c + 7 = 32$
29. $9m + 5 = 41$
30. $8n + 5 = 53$
31. $6x + 7 = 13$
32. $3y + 8 = 29$
33. $8t + 9 = 41$
34. $3z + 8 = 17$
35. $4a + 11 = 19$
36. $5b + 13 = 38$
37. $7c + 11 = 60$
38. $9d + 16 = 34$
39. $12p + 13 = 85$
40. $11q + 16 = 60$

41. $3x - 11 = 10$
42. $4x - 9 = 3$
43. $6y - 5 = 1$
44. $7y - 2 = 12$
45. $6z - 7 = 11$
46. $2t - 3 = 15$
47. $3a - 5 = 16$
48. $5b - 8 = 17$
49. $4c - 5 = 19$
50. $8d - 9 = 15$
51. $5m - 7 = 18$
52. $7n - 8 = 27$
53. $9p - 8 = 28$
54. $6q - 7 = 47$
55. $8x - 12 = 20$
56. $7x - 10 = 25$
57. $6y - 15 = 21$
58. $9y - 20 = 34$
59. $12z - 14 = 22$
60. $11t - 15 = 40$

Often like terms have to be collected before an equation can be solved.

Example 3

Solve the following equations.

a) $6x - 3x + 2x = 10$
b) $5a + 5 + 3a = 21$

a) $6x - 3x + 2x = 10$

$\Rightarrow \qquad 3x + 2x = 10$

$\Rightarrow \qquad\qquad 5x = 10$ (collect like terms)

So, $\qquad\qquad x = 2$ (divide by 5)

b) $5a + 5 + 3a = 21$

$\Rightarrow \qquad 8a + 5 = 21$ (collect like terms)

$\Rightarrow \qquad\qquad 8a = 16$ (subtract 5)

$\Rightarrow \qquad\qquad a = 2$ (divide by 8)

Exercise 48

Solve the following equations.

 1. $6x + 3x + 2x = 33$
 2. $5y + 2y + y = 56$
 3. $3p + 4p - 2p = 20$
 4. $5q + 3q - 6q = 16$
 5. $6r + 4r - r = 36$
 6. $8s + 2s - 9s = 12$
 7. $8a - 3a + 2a = 21$
 8. $9b - 6b + 4b = 35$
 9. $12c - 5c + 2c = 54$
10. $5d - d + 4d = 40$

11. $9m - 3m - 2m = 8$
12. $12n - 2n - 7n = 15$
13. $11u - 4u - u = 30$
14. $15v - 5v - 9v = 7$
15. $4a + 7 + 2a = 25$
16. $6b + 5 + 3b = 50$
17. $3c + 9 + 5c = 17$
18. $7d + 15 + d = 55$
19. $3p - 8 + 2p = 22$
20. $5q - 3 + 3q = 29$

21. $4r - 11 + 5r = 25$
22. $9s - 12 + 2s = 21$
23. $9x + 5 - 3x = 23$
24. $12y + 7 - 4y = 63$
25. $20t + 9 - 12t = 33$
26. $11z + 15 - 7z = 35$
27. $9m - 7 - 3m = 5$
28. $12n - 8 - 5n = 13$
29. $11v - 12 - 4v = 9$
30. $15u - 15 - 7u = 17$

5.3 ALGEBRAIC FRACTIONS

$\dfrac{a}{2}; \quad \dfrac{3}{x}; \quad \dfrac{b}{y}$

e.g. $\dfrac{a}{2} = \dfrac{a \times 2}{2 \times 2} = \dfrac{2a}{4}$

Terms such as these are called algebraic fractions.

$\dfrac{3}{x} = \dfrac{3 \times x}{x \times x} = \dfrac{3x}{x^2}$

Calculations with algebraic fractions use the same rules as ordinary fractions.

$\dfrac{6x}{10} = \dfrac{6x \div 2}{10 \div 2} = \dfrac{3x}{5}$

The value of an algebraic fraction is not changed when both the numerator and the denominator are multiplied or divided by the same number.

Example 1

Copy and complete the following.

a) $\dfrac{x}{3} = \dfrac{}{6}$ b) $\dfrac{3}{a} = \dfrac{15}{}$

c) $\dfrac{x}{y} = \dfrac{x^2}{}$

a) $\dfrac{x}{3} = \dfrac{x \times 2}{3 \times 2} = \dfrac{2x}{6}$

b) $\dfrac{3}{a} = \dfrac{3 \times 5}{a \times 5} = \dfrac{15}{5a}$

c) $\dfrac{x}{y} = \dfrac{x \times x}{y \times x} = \dfrac{x^2}{xy}$

Example 2

Copy and complete the following.

a) $\dfrac{2x}{8} = \dfrac{}{4}$ b) $\dfrac{14}{7b} = \dfrac{2}{}$

c) $\dfrac{y}{2y} = \dfrac{1}{}$

a) $\dfrac{2x}{8} = \dfrac{2x \div 2}{8 \div 2} = \dfrac{x}{4}$

b) $\dfrac{14}{7b} = \dfrac{14 \div 7}{7b \div 7} = \dfrac{2}{b}$

c) $\dfrac{y}{2y} = \dfrac{y \div y}{2y \div y} = \dfrac{1}{2}$

Exercise 49

Copy and complete the following.

1. $\dfrac{x}{4} = \dfrac{}{8}$ 2. $\dfrac{x}{5} = \dfrac{}{15}$ 3. $\dfrac{a}{3} = \dfrac{}{3b}$

4. $\dfrac{c}{2} = \dfrac{}{2d}$ 5. $\dfrac{m}{5} = \dfrac{}{5m}$ 6. $\dfrac{n}{8} = \dfrac{}{8n}$

7. $\dfrac{5}{p} = \dfrac{20}{}$ 8. $\dfrac{6}{q} = \dfrac{18}{}$ 9. $\dfrac{2}{u} = \dfrac{2v}{}$

10. $\dfrac{4}{x} = \dfrac{4y}{}$ 11. $\dfrac{3}{z} = \dfrac{3z}{}$ 12. $\dfrac{7}{t} = \dfrac{7t}{}$

13. $\dfrac{x}{y} = \dfrac{}{3y}$ 14. $\dfrac{a}{b} = \dfrac{}{5b}$ 15. $\dfrac{p}{q} = \dfrac{}{qr}$

16. $\dfrac{x}{y} = \dfrac{}{yz}$ 17. $\dfrac{r}{s} = \dfrac{}{s^2}$ 18. $\dfrac{c}{d} = \dfrac{}{d^2}$

19. $\dfrac{u}{v} = \dfrac{}{uv}$ 20. $\dfrac{m}{n} = \dfrac{}{mn}$ 21. $\dfrac{p}{q} = \dfrac{5p}{}$

22. $\dfrac{x}{y} = \dfrac{9x}{}$ 23. $\dfrac{a}{b} = \dfrac{ac}{}$ 24. $\dfrac{r}{s} = \dfrac{rt}{}$

25. $\dfrac{p}{q} = \dfrac{pq}{}$ 26. $\dfrac{x}{y} = \dfrac{xy}{}$ 27. $\dfrac{a}{b} = \dfrac{a^2}{}$

28. $\dfrac{d}{e} = \dfrac{d^2}{}$ 29. $\dfrac{6x}{8} = \dfrac{}{4}$ 30. $\dfrac{10y}{12} = \dfrac{}{6}$

31. $\dfrac{2z}{10} = \dfrac{}{5}$ 32. $\dfrac{8a}{6} = \dfrac{}{3}$ 33. $\dfrac{6b}{4} = \dfrac{}{2}$

34. $\dfrac{6t}{15} = \dfrac{}{5}$ 35. $\dfrac{9c}{12} = \dfrac{}{4}$ 36. $\dfrac{3d}{9} = \dfrac{}{3}$

37. $\dfrac{15e}{12} = \dfrac{}{4}$ 38. $\dfrac{10}{16m} = \dfrac{5}{}$ 39. $\dfrac{8}{10n} = \dfrac{4}{}$

40. $\dfrac{14}{8p} = \dfrac{7}{}$ 41. $\dfrac{4}{2q} = \dfrac{2}{}$ 42. $\dfrac{6}{9r} = \dfrac{2}{}$

43. $\dfrac{12}{15s} = \dfrac{4}{}$ 44. $\dfrac{8}{20u} = \dfrac{2}{}$ 45. $\dfrac{4}{16v} = \dfrac{1}{}$

46. $\dfrac{4x}{6x} = \dfrac{}{3}$ 47. $\dfrac{6y}{10y} = \dfrac{}{5}$ 48. $\dfrac{12z}{10z} = \dfrac{}{5}$

49. $\dfrac{2t}{12t} = \dfrac{}{6}$ 50. $\dfrac{9u}{15u} = \dfrac{}{5}$ 51. $\dfrac{9v}{6v} = \dfrac{}{2}$

52. $\dfrac{12m}{4m} = \dfrac{}{}$ 53. $\dfrac{16n}{20n} = \dfrac{}{5}$ 54. $\dfrac{4a}{10a} = \dfrac{2}{}$

55. $\dfrac{2b}{8b} = \dfrac{1}{}$ 56. $\dfrac{10c}{6c} = \dfrac{5}{}$ 57. $\dfrac{10d}{15d} = \dfrac{2}{}$

58. $\dfrac{12e}{16e} = \dfrac{3}{}$ 59. $\dfrac{20m}{8m} = \dfrac{5}{}$ 60. $\dfrac{3n}{12n} = \dfrac{1}{}$

Algebraic fractions (like common fractions) are always written in their simplest form.

Example 3

Write each in its simplest form.

a) $\dfrac{4}{8x}$ b) $\dfrac{10a}{15}$ c) $\dfrac{12x}{18y}$

a) The numerator and the denominator are both divisible by 4.

So, $\dfrac{4}{8x} = \dfrac{4 \div 4}{8x \div 4} = \dfrac{1}{2x}$

b) The numerator and the denominator are both divisible by 5.

So, $\dfrac{10a}{15} = \dfrac{10a \div 5}{15 \div 5} = \dfrac{2a}{3}$

c) The numerator and the denominator are both divisible by 6.

So, $\dfrac{12x}{18y} = \dfrac{12x \div 6}{18y \div 6} = \dfrac{2x}{3y}$

Algebraic fractions can only be added or subtracted when they have a common denominator.

Example 4

Add the following.

a) $\dfrac{3}{x} + \dfrac{2}{x}$ b) $\dfrac{2a}{5} + \dfrac{a}{5}$

c) $\dfrac{3x}{a} + \dfrac{y}{a}$ d) $\dfrac{x}{8} + \dfrac{x}{8}$

a) $\dfrac{3}{x} + \dfrac{2}{x} = \dfrac{3+2}{x} = \dfrac{5}{x}$

b) $\dfrac{2a}{5} + \dfrac{a}{5} = \dfrac{2a+a}{5} = \dfrac{3a}{5}$

c) $\dfrac{3x}{a} + \dfrac{y}{a} = \dfrac{3x+y}{a}$

d) $\dfrac{x}{8} + \dfrac{x}{8} = \dfrac{x+x}{8}$

$= \dfrac{2x}{8}$

$= \dfrac{2x \div 2}{8 \div 2} = \dfrac{x}{4}$

Exercise 50

Write each in its simplest form.

1. $\dfrac{6a}{10}$ 2. $\dfrac{10b}{12}$ 3. $\dfrac{4c}{6}$ 4. $\dfrac{8}{10x}$

5. $\dfrac{6}{8y}$ 6. $\dfrac{2}{6z}$ 7. $\dfrac{4m}{10n}$ 8. $\dfrac{10p}{16q}$

9. $\dfrac{2u}{8v}$ 10. $\dfrac{6c}{15}$ 11. $\dfrac{9d}{12}$ 12. $\dfrac{6}{9r}$

13. $\dfrac{3}{12s}$ 14. $\dfrac{9a}{15b}$ 15. $\dfrac{3x}{6y}$ 16. $\dfrac{8p}{12}$

17. $\dfrac{12q}{20}$ 18. $\dfrac{8}{20m}$ 19. $\dfrac{4}{16n}$ 20. $\dfrac{16u}{20v}$

21. $\dfrac{12y}{16z}$ 22. $\dfrac{4r}{12s}$ 23. $\dfrac{10a}{15}$ 24. $\dfrac{5}{20b}$

25. $\dfrac{15m}{20n}$ 26. $\dfrac{10x}{25y}$ 27. $\dfrac{18c}{30d}$ 28. $\dfrac{6p}{24q}$

29. $\dfrac{24u}{40}$ 30. $\dfrac{8}{48v}$

Exercise 51

Add the following.

1. $\dfrac{3}{a} + \dfrac{5}{a}$ 2. $\dfrac{2}{b} + \dfrac{7}{b}$ 3. $\dfrac{4}{c} + \dfrac{8}{c}$

4. $\dfrac{3}{2x} + \dfrac{9}{2x}$ 5. $\dfrac{7}{2y} + \dfrac{13}{2y}$ 6. $\dfrac{4}{3p} + \dfrac{11}{3p}$

7. $\dfrac{13}{3q} + \dfrac{8}{3q}$ 8. $\dfrac{4}{5r} + \dfrac{6}{5r}$ 9. $\dfrac{2a}{5} + \dfrac{4a}{5}$

10. $\dfrac{3b}{7} + \dfrac{5b}{7}$ 11. $\dfrac{4c}{9} + \dfrac{c}{9}$ 12. $\dfrac{4m}{3} + \dfrac{5m}{3}$

13. $\dfrac{9n}{4} + \dfrac{7n}{4}$ 14. $\dfrac{13t}{6} + \dfrac{17t}{6}$ 15. $\dfrac{9z}{5} + \dfrac{z}{5}$

16. $\dfrac{3p}{10} + \dfrac{2p}{10}$ 17. $\dfrac{3s}{40} + \dfrac{7s}{40}$ 18. $\dfrac{q}{9} + \dfrac{2q}{9}$

19. $\dfrac{3r}{24} + \dfrac{r}{24}$ 20. $\dfrac{2a}{5} + \dfrac{3b}{5}$ 21. $\dfrac{5c}{6} + \dfrac{4d}{6}$

22. $\dfrac{4m}{3} + \dfrac{n}{3}$ 23. $\dfrac{5p}{r} + \dfrac{3q}{r}$ 24. $\dfrac{2x}{z} + \dfrac{7y}{z}$

Example 5

Subtract the following.

a) $\dfrac{4}{a} - \dfrac{3}{a}$ b) $\dfrac{4c}{7} - \dfrac{2c}{7}$ c) $\dfrac{3y}{8} - \dfrac{y}{8}$

a) $\dfrac{4}{a} - \dfrac{3}{a} = \dfrac{4-3}{a} = \dfrac{1}{a}$

b) $\dfrac{4c}{7} - \dfrac{2c}{7} = \dfrac{4c-2c}{7} = \dfrac{2c}{7}$

c) $\dfrac{3y}{8} - \dfrac{y}{8} = \dfrac{3y-y}{8} = \dfrac{2y}{8} = \dfrac{2y \div 2}{8 \div 2} = \dfrac{y}{4}$

Exercise 52

Subtract the following.

1. $\dfrac{7}{m} - \dfrac{4}{m}$ 2. $\dfrac{9}{n} - \dfrac{3}{n}$ 3. $\dfrac{12}{t} - \dfrac{2}{t}$

4. $\dfrac{7}{2a} - \dfrac{3}{2a}$ 5. $\dfrac{9}{2b} - \dfrac{1}{2b}$ 6. $\dfrac{11}{3x} - \dfrac{5}{3x}$

7. $\dfrac{13}{3y} - \dfrac{4}{3y}$ 8. $\dfrac{15}{4z} - \dfrac{7}{4z}$ 9. $\dfrac{7p}{3} - \dfrac{2p}{3}$

10. $\dfrac{9q}{5} - \dfrac{3q}{5}$ 11. $\dfrac{5r}{9} - \dfrac{r}{9}$ 12. $\dfrac{9a}{2} - \dfrac{3a}{2}$

13. $\dfrac{11b}{5} - \dfrac{b}{5}$ 14. $\dfrac{15c}{4} - \dfrac{3c}{4}$ 15. $\dfrac{11d}{3} - \dfrac{8d}{3}$

16. $\dfrac{7m}{8} - \dfrac{3m}{8}$ 17. $\dfrac{9n}{20} - \dfrac{7n}{20}$ 18. $\dfrac{11u}{12} - \dfrac{7u}{12}$

19. $\dfrac{7v}{30} - \dfrac{v}{30}$ 20. $\dfrac{4x}{5} - \dfrac{3y}{5}$ 21. $\dfrac{7p}{3} - \dfrac{5q}{3}$

22. $\dfrac{m}{8} - \dfrac{9n}{8}$ 23. $\dfrac{3a}{c} - \dfrac{2b}{c}$ 24. $\dfrac{6p}{r} - \dfrac{q}{r}$

Example 6

Simplify:

a) $\dfrac{a}{2} + \dfrac{a}{3}$ b) $\dfrac{y}{3} - \dfrac{y}{9}$

c) $\dfrac{3x}{5} + \dfrac{x}{10}$ d) $\dfrac{5a}{6} - \dfrac{a}{2}$

a) $\dfrac{a}{2} + \dfrac{a}{3} = \dfrac{a \times 3}{2 \times 3} + \dfrac{a \times 2}{3 \times 2}$ (as the common denominator is 6)

$= \dfrac{3a}{6} + \dfrac{2a}{6}$

$= \dfrac{3a + 2a}{6} = \dfrac{5a}{6}$

b) $\dfrac{y}{3} - \dfrac{y}{9} = \dfrac{y \times 3}{3 \times 3} - \dfrac{y}{9}$ (as the common denominator is 9)

$= \dfrac{3y}{9} - \dfrac{y}{9}$

$= \dfrac{3y - y}{9} = \dfrac{2y}{9}$

c) $\dfrac{3x}{5} + \dfrac{x}{10} = \dfrac{3x \times 2}{5 \times 2} + \dfrac{x}{10}$ (as the common denominator is 10)

$= \dfrac{6x}{10} + \dfrac{x}{10}$

$= \dfrac{6x + x}{10} = \dfrac{7x}{10}$

d) $\dfrac{5a}{6} - \dfrac{a}{2} = \dfrac{5a}{6} - \dfrac{a \times 3}{2 \times 3}$ (as the common denominator is 6)

$= \dfrac{5a}{6} - \dfrac{3a}{6}$

$= \dfrac{5a - 3a}{6} = \dfrac{2a}{6} = \dfrac{a}{3}$

Exercise 53

Simplify:

1. $\dfrac{a}{4} + \dfrac{a}{8}$ 2. $\dfrac{b}{5} + \dfrac{b}{10}$ 3. $\dfrac{c}{3} + \dfrac{c}{12}$

4. $\dfrac{d}{2} + \dfrac{d}{6}$ 5. $\dfrac{e}{2} + \dfrac{e}{10}$ 6. $\dfrac{m}{3} + \dfrac{m}{4}$

7. $\dfrac{n}{3} + \dfrac{n}{5}$ 8. $\dfrac{p}{4} + \dfrac{p}{5}$ 9. $\dfrac{q}{10} + \dfrac{q}{15}$

10. $\dfrac{r}{6} + \dfrac{r}{10}$ 11. $\dfrac{x}{2} + \dfrac{3x}{10}$ 12. $\dfrac{y}{5} + \dfrac{11y}{20}$

13. $\dfrac{z}{4} + \dfrac{5z}{12}$ 14. $\dfrac{3u}{4} + \dfrac{u}{20}$ 15. $\dfrac{3v}{10} + \dfrac{v}{30}$

16. $\dfrac{a}{3} + \dfrac{2a}{5}$ **17.** $\dfrac{3b}{4} + \dfrac{b}{6}$ **18.** $\dfrac{c}{6} + \dfrac{3c}{10}$ **28.** $\dfrac{p}{4} - \dfrac{p}{6}$ **29.** $\dfrac{q}{6} - \dfrac{q}{15}$ **30.** $\dfrac{r}{12} - \dfrac{r}{20}$

19. $\dfrac{d}{10} + \dfrac{11d}{15}$ **20.** $\dfrac{e}{12} + \dfrac{4e}{15}$ **21.** $\dfrac{x}{2} - \dfrac{x}{8}$ **31.** $\dfrac{3a}{4} - \dfrac{a}{12}$ **32.** $\dfrac{5b}{6} - \dfrac{b}{30}$ **33.** $\dfrac{9c}{10} - \dfrac{c}{40}$

22. $\dfrac{y}{3} - \dfrac{y}{9}$ **23.** $\dfrac{z}{4} - \dfrac{z}{12}$ **24.** $\dfrac{t}{4} - \dfrac{t}{20}$ **34.** $\dfrac{3d}{10} - \dfrac{d}{20}$ **35.** $\dfrac{e}{4} - \dfrac{3e}{20}$ **36.** $\dfrac{3p}{4} - \dfrac{p}{5}$

25. $\dfrac{u}{10} - \dfrac{u}{30}$ **26.** $\dfrac{m}{2} - \dfrac{m}{5}$ **27.** $\dfrac{n}{3} - \dfrac{n}{10}$ **37.** $\dfrac{5q}{6} - \dfrac{q}{4}$ **38.** $\dfrac{r}{2} - \dfrac{2r}{5}$ **39.** $\dfrac{7x}{10} - \dfrac{x}{6}$

5.4 CHANGE OF SUBJECT

$$A = LB; \quad L = \dfrac{A}{B}; \quad \dfrac{A}{L} = B$$

These are all arrangements of the same formula, but the subject of each is different. To change the subject of a formula, a similar method is used to that for solving an equation.

Example 1

a) Make x the subject of $y = mx$

$$y = mx$$

$\Rightarrow \quad \dfrac{y}{m} = x$ (divide both sides by m)

b) Rearrange $C = 2\pi r$ to find the value of r

$$C = 2\pi r$$

$\Rightarrow \quad \dfrac{C}{2\pi} = r$ (divide both sides by 2π)

Exercise 54

1. Make b the subject of $A = bh$
2. Rearrange $V = Al$ to find l
3. If $P = VI$, find the value of V
4. Transpose $v = lf$ to make f the subject
5. Make a the subject of $v = at$
6. If $q = It$, find the value of t
7. Transpose $U = Pt$ to make P the subject
8. Rearrange $F = ma$ to find a
9. $m = Zq$ Change the subject to Z

10. Make V the subject of $k = PV$
11. Find F when $W = Fd$
12. Rearrange $P = hdg$ to find d
13. If $I = PrT$, find the value of P
14. Transpose $W = mgh$ to make h the subject
15. Make b the subject of $V = lbh$
16. If $A = \pi Dl$, find the value of D
17. Rearrange $A = 4lb$ to find b
18. $S = 4bh$ Change the subject to b
19. Find l when $A = 3ls$
20. Make s the subject of $v^2 = 2as$

Example 2

a) If $r = \dfrac{D}{2}$, find the value of D

$$r = \dfrac{D}{2}$$

$\Rightarrow \quad 2r = D$ (multiply both sides by 2)

b) Find C when $\pi = \dfrac{C}{D}$

$$\pi = \dfrac{C}{D}$$

$\Rightarrow \quad \pi D = C$ (multiply both sides by D)

c) Make H the subject of $A = \dfrac{BH}{2}$

$$A = \dfrac{BH}{2}$$

$\Rightarrow \quad 2A = BH$ (multiply both sides by 2)

$$\dfrac{2A}{B} = H \quad \text{(divide both sides by } B)$$

Exercise 55

1. Find x when $n = \dfrac{x}{y}$

2. Make V the subject of $R = \dfrac{V}{I}$

3. If $s = \dfrac{d}{t}$, find the value of d

4. Transpose $L = \dfrac{H}{m}$ to make H the subject

5. Rearrange $D = \dfrac{m}{V}$ to find m

6. Find v when $m = \dfrac{v}{u}$

7. $P = \dfrac{F}{A}$ Rearrange to find F

8. Make P the subject of $k = \dfrac{P}{T}$

9. If $c = \dfrac{V}{T}$, find the value of V

10. Find p when $l = \dfrac{p}{4}$

11. Rearrange $s = \dfrac{q}{3}$ to find q

12. Make r the subject of $b = \dfrac{r}{15}$

13. Find l when $L = \dfrac{l}{10}$

14. $W = \dfrac{D}{7}$ Rearrange to find D

15. Make M the subject of $Y = \dfrac{M}{12}$

16. If $h = \dfrac{m}{60}$, find the value of m

17. Transpose $D = \dfrac{h}{24}$ to find h

18. Find m when $M = \dfrac{m}{100}$

19. Make v the subject of $V = \dfrac{v}{1000}$

20. Rearrange $d = \dfrac{l}{50}$ to find l

21. Find a) x, b) y, when $m = \dfrac{xy}{10}$

22. Find a) u, b) v, when $a = \dfrac{uv}{50}$

23. If $t = \dfrac{pq}{25}$, find a) p, b) q

24. If $V = \dfrac{Ah}{3}$, find a) A, b) h

25. $R = \dfrac{PV}{T}$ Rearrange to find a) P, b) V

26. If $a = \dfrac{pqr}{5}$ make the subject a) p, b) q, c) r

27. Find a) x, b) y, c) z, when $t = \dfrac{xyz}{20}$

28. Find a) b, b) h, c) l, when $V = \dfrac{bhl}{2}$

29. Rearrange $V = \dfrac{abh}{3}$ to find a) a, b) b, c) h

30. $I = \dfrac{PRt}{100}$ Rearrange to find a) P b) R, c) t

Example 3

a) Make a the subject when $a + b = 180°$.

$$a + b = 180°$$
$$\Rightarrow \qquad a = 180° - b$$

(subtract b from both sides)

b) Find h when $H = bt + h$.

$$H = bt + h$$
$$\Rightarrow \qquad H - bt = h$$

(subtract bt from both sides)

c) If $v - u = at$, find the value of v.

$$v - u = at$$
$$\Rightarrow \qquad v = at + u$$

(add u to both sides)

Exercise 56

1. Make m the subject of $m + n = u$
2. Rearrange $p + q = z$ to find p
3. If $a + b = t$, find the value of a
4. Transpose $x + y = 360°$ to make y the subject
5. Make b the subject of $p = b + c$
6. If $n = u + v$, find the value of u
7. Transpose $90° = r + s$ to make s the subject
8. Rearrange $q - r = t$ to find q
9. $b - c = v$ Change the subject to b
10. Make y the subject of $y - z = m$
11. Find a when $x = a - b$
12. Rearrange $n = p - q$ to find p

13. If $z = d - e$, find the value of d
14. Transpose $a + bt = A$ to make a the subject
15. Make p the subject of $p + qz = P$
16. If $V = v + ct$, find the value of v
17. Rearrange $P = p + at$ to find p
18. $H = h + kd$ Change the subject to h
19. Find c when $y = mx + c$
20. Make V the subject of $E = rI + V$
21. If $180° = 2y + z$, find the value of z
22. Rearrange $m - nt = M$ to find m
23. Find u when $u - vh = U$
24. Transpose $H = h - vt$ to make h the subject
25. Make k the subject of $S = k - mt$

11. $360° = 3m + n$ Change the subject to m
12. Make t the subject of $u = 4t - v$
13. Find z when $a = 10z - b$
14. Rearrange $x = 2a + 3b$ to find a) a, b) b
15. If $y = 3m + 8n$, find the value of a) m, b) n
16. Find a) w, b) l, when $s = 8w + 4l$
17. Find a) x, b) y, when $900° = 5x + 2y$
18. If $p = 2l + \pi d$, find a) l, b) d
19. Make b the subject of $t = 4b - 5c$
20. Find p if $z = 6p - 7q$
21. If $a = 3b + mn$, make the subject a) b, b) m, c) n
22. If $p = 5q + uv$, make the subject a) q, b) u, c) v
23. Make v the subject of $u = 6v - xy$
24. Find a) p, b) q, when $m = pq - 4n$
25. Find a) r, b) s, when $c = rs - 9d$
26. a) Make a the subject of the formula $v = u + at$ and work out the value of a if $v = 45, u = 15$ and $t = 3$.
    b) Make t the subject of the formula $v = u + at$ and work out the value of t if $v = 12, u = 4$ and $a = 2$.
27. a) Make r the subject of the formula $E = V + rI$ and work out the value of r if $E = 24, V = 9$ and $I = 5$.
    b) Make I the subject of the formula $E = V + rI$ and work out the value of I if $E = 30, V = 14$ and $r = 8$.
28. a) Make a the subject of the formula $c = ab - d$ and work out the value of a if $c = 27, d = 29$ and $b = 8$.
    b) Make b the subject of the formula $c = ab - d$ and work out the value of b if $c = 65, d = 67$ and $a = 11$.
29. a) Make m the subject of the formula $p = mn - q$ and work out the value of m if $p = 14\frac{1}{2}, q = 15\frac{1}{2}$ and $n = 6$.
    b) Make n the subject of the formula $p = mn - q$ and work out the value of n if $p = 5\frac{1}{4}, q = 6\frac{3}{4}$ and $m = 3$.
30. Rearrange the formula $P = p + kt$ so that k is the subject and find the value of k if $P = 95, p = 70$ and $t = 100$.

Example 4

a) Find a when $v = u + at$

$$v = u + at$$

$\Rightarrow \qquad v - u = at$

(subtract u from both sides)

$\Rightarrow \qquad \dfrac{v - u}{t} = a$

(divide both sides by t)

b) Make L the subject of $P = 2L + 2B$

$$P = 2L + 2B$$

$\Rightarrow \qquad P - 2B = 2L$

(subtract $2B$ from both sides)

$\Rightarrow \qquad \dfrac{P - 2B}{2} = L$

(divide both sides by 2)

Exercise 57

1. Find m when $p = q + mn$
2. Make x the subject of $a = b + xy$
3. Rearrange $E = V + rI$ to find r
4. If $y = mx + c$, find the value of m
5. Transpose $z = st + k$ to make s the subject
6. Make a the subject of $m = ab - n$
7. Find p if $r = pq - s$
8. If $c = d + 2r$, find the value of r
9. Transpose $x = y + 5t$ to make t the subject
10. Rearrange $p = 2s + b$ to find s

The change in position of an object is known as a *transformation*. In Book 3 we looked at reflection in which an object is transformed to its mirror image.
Rotation is another kind of transformation. The object is rotated about a fixed point (the centre of rotation) to form the image.

Example 1

Copy the shape below onto graph paper or squared paper.

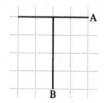

Then draw the image formed by rotating the object.

a) 90° clockwise about A

b) 90° clockwise about B

a)
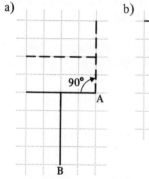
b)
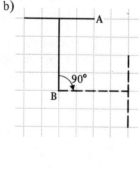

Exercise 58

Copy the object shown in each question onto graph paper or squared paper. Then draw the image formed by rotating the object clockwise through 90° about i) A; ii) B. Show a separate diagram for each rotation.

1.
2.
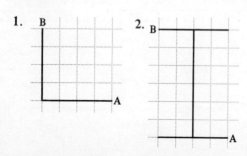

3.
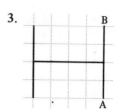
4.
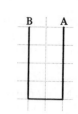

5.
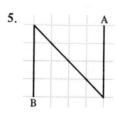
6.

7.
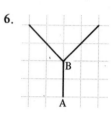
8.

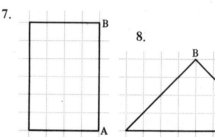

9.
10.
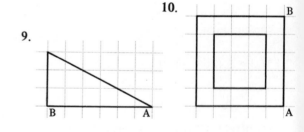

Example 2

Copy the triangle ABC onto graph paper or squared paper.

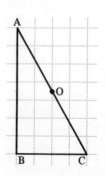

Then draw the image formed

a) when the triangle is reflected along the line AC,

b) when the triangle is rotated through 180° about O, the mid-point of AC.

Name the figure produced in each case.

a) b)

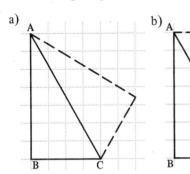

a) The shape is a kite.
b) The shape is a rectangle.

Exercise 59

For questions **1** to **4**, copy the triangle ABC onto graph paper or squared paper. Then draw the image of the triangle formed:
a) by reflection in the line BC,
b) by rotation through 180° about O.
Name the figure produced in each case.

1. 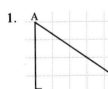   2.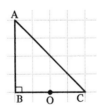

3. 4.

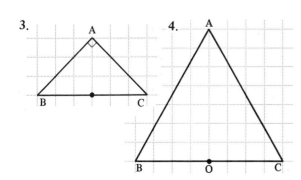

5. Make two copies of the figure ABCD on graph paper or squared paper.

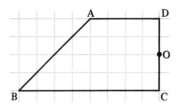

Then draw the image of the shape formed:
a) by reflection in the line BC,
b) by rotation through 180° about O.
Name the figure produced in each case.

For questions **6** to **8**, copy the figure onto graph paper or squared paper. Then draw the image of the shape formed by rotation through 90° about O, the centre of the figure.

6. 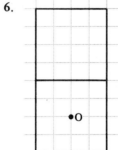   7.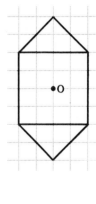

8.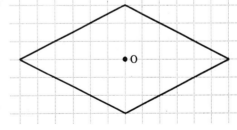

9. The illustration shows the equilateral triangle ABC and its image after rotation.

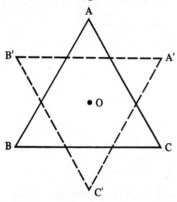

Has the triangle been rotated through 30°, 45° or 60°?

10. The illustration shows the square ABCD and its image after rotation.

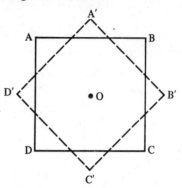

Has the square been rotated through 30°, 45° or 60°?

6.2 SETS

You should by now be familiar with the following symbols.

& universal set   ∩ intersection of sets

∪ union of sets   A′ the complement of set A
                                    i.e. the elements *not* in set A

When A = {letters of the alphabet}, the number of elements in set A is 26. This is written $n(A) = 26$

Example 1

If & = {1, 2, 3, 4, 5, 6, 7, 8, 9, 10}
    A = {2, 3, 5, 7} and B = {1, 3, 5, 7, 9},
find the value of the following.

a) $n(A)$ b) $n(B')$ c) $n(A \cap B)$ d) $n(A' \cup B')$

a) A = {2, 3, 5, 7}; so $n(A) = 4$
b) B′ = {2, 4, 6, 8, 10}; so $n(B') = 5$
c) A ∩ B = {3, 5, 7}; so $n(A \cap B) = 3$
d) A′ = {1, 4, 6, 8, 9, 10}; B′ = {2, 4, 6, 8, 10}
   ∴ A′ ∪ B′ = {1, 2, 4, 6, 8, 9, 10}; so $n(A' \cup B') = 7$

Exercise 60

For questions **1** to **4**, find the value of the following.

a) $n(A)$ b) $n(B)$ c) $n(A \cap B)$ d) $n(A \cup B)$

1. $\& = \{1, 2, 3, 4, 5, 6, 7, 8, 9, 10\}$; $A = \{1, 2, 4, 8\}$; $B = \{1, 4, 9\}$.
2. $\& = \{1, 2, 3, 4, 5, 6, 7, 8, 9, 10\}$; $A = \{1, 2, 3, 6\}$; $B = \{1, 4, 9\}$.
3. $\& = \{1, 2, 3, 4, 5, 6, 7, 8, 9, 10\}$; $A = \{1, 3, 9\}$; $B = \{1, 4, 9\}$.
4. $\& = \{1, 2, 3, 4, 5, 6, 7, 8, 9, 10\}$; $A = \{1, 2, 4\}$; $B = \{1, 3, 6, 10\}$.

For questions **5** to **8**, find the value of the following.

a) $n(A')$ b) $n(B')$ c) $n(A' \cap B')$ d) $n(A' \cup B')$

5. $\& = \{1, 2, 3, 4, 5, 6, 7, 8, 9, 10\}$; $A = \{1, 2, 4, 8\}$; $B = \{2, 4, 6, 8, 10\}$.
6. $\& = \{1, 2, 3, 4, 5, 6, 7, 8, 9, 10\}$; $A = \{1, 2, 3, 6\}$; $B = \{2, 4, 6, 8, 10\}$.
7. $\& = \{1, 2, 3, 4, 5, 6, 7, 8, 9, 10\}$; $A = \{1, 3, 9\}$; $B = \{1, 3, 6, 10\}$.
8. $\& = \{1, 2, 3, 4, 5, 6, 7, 8, 9, 10\}$; $A = \{1, 2, 5\}$; $B = \{1, 4, 9\}$.

For questions **9** and **10**, find the value of the following.

a) $n(A)$ b) $n(B)$ c) $n(A \cap B)$ d) $n(A')$
e) $n(B')$ f) $n(A' \cap B')$

9. $\& = \{$London, Liverpool, Hull, Southampton$\}$;
   $A = \{$London, Liverpool$\}$; $B = \{$Liverpool, Hull$\}$.
10. $\& = \{$Blackpool, Bournemouth, Brighton, Ramsgate, Scarborough, Southend$\}$;
    $A = \{$Blackpool, Bournemouth, Brighton$\}$; $B = \{$Brighton, Ramsgate Southend$\}$.

Example 2

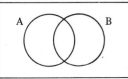

Draw a diagram similar to that on the left for each of the following;
then shade in the part of the diagram required to show:

a) $A \cap B$ b) $A \cup B$ c) A' d) $(A \cup B)'$

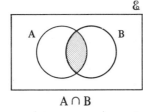

$A \cap B$

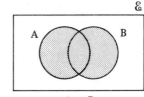

$A \cup B$

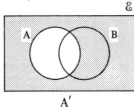

A'

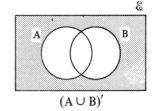

$(A \cup B)'$

Exercise 61

1. Draw a diagram similar to that on the left for each of the following: then shade
   in the part of the diagram required to show
   a) A b) B c) B' d) $(A \cap B)'$

&

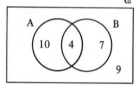

2. Draw a diagram similar to that on the left for each of the following: then shade in the part of the diagram required to show:

a) A   b) B   c) A∪B   d) A′   e) B′   f) (A∪B)′

3. Give *two* expressions for the shaded region in each of the diagrams below.

a)   &   b)   &   c)   &   d)   &

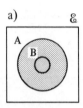 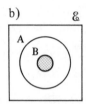 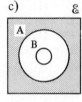 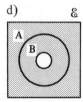

Example 3

&

The Venn diagram on the left shows the number of elements in each of the subsets of the universal set & where

& = {pupils in class 2Y};

A = {pupils who play the piano};

B = {pupils who sing in the school choir}

a) How many pupils are there in class 2Y?

$$n(\&) = 10 + 4 + 7 + 9 = 30$$

b) How many pupils play the piano?

$$n(A) = 10 + 4 = 14$$

c) How many pupils sing in the school choir?

$$n(B) = 7 + 4 = 11$$

d) How many pupils both play the piano and sing in the school choir?

$$n(A \cap B) = 4$$

e) How many pupils do *not* play the piano?

$$n(A') = 7 + 9 = 16$$

f) How many pupils do *not* sing in the school choir?

$$n(B') = 10 + 9 = 19$$

g) How many pupils neither play the piano nor sing in the school choir?

$$n(A \cup B)' = 9$$

h) How many pupils play the piano but do not sing in the school choir?

$$n(A \cap B') = 10 \text{ because 4 sing in the school choir}$$

i) How many pupils sing in the school choir but do not play the piano?

$$n(B \cap A') = 7 \text{ because 4 play the piano}$$

Exercise 62

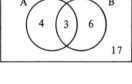

&

1. The Venn diagram on the left shows the number of elements in each of the subsets of the universal set & where:
   & = {girls in class 4A}; A = {girls with blonde hair}; B = {girls with blue eyes}
   a) How many girls are there in class 4A?
   b) How many girls have blonde hair?
   c) How many girls have blue eyes?
   d) How many girls have both blonde hair and blue eyes?
   e) How many girls do not have blonde hair?
   f) How many girls do not have blue eyes?
   g) How many girls have neither blonde hair nor blue eyes?
   h) How many girls have blonde hair but not blue eyes?
   i) How many girls have blue eyes but not blonde hair?

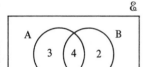

&

2. The Venn diagram on the left shows the number of elements in each of the subsets of the universal set & where:
   & = {boys in class 5C}; A = {boys in the school football team};
   B = {boys in the school cross-country team}
   a) How many boys are there in class 5C?
   b) How many boys play in the school football team?
   c) How many boys run in the school cross-country team?
   d) How many boys are in both the football and cross-country teams?
   e) How many boys do not play in the football team?
   f) How many boys do not run in the cross-country team?
   g) How many boys are in neither the football team nor the cross-country team?
   h) How many boys are in the football team but not in the cross country team?
   i) How many boys are in the cross-country team but not in the football team?

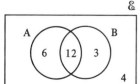

&

3. The Venn diagram on the left shows the number of elements in each of the subsets of the universal set & where:
   & = {boys in class 3B}; A = {boys in the school cricket team};
   B = {boys in the school athletics team}
   a) How many boys are there in class 3B?
   b) How many boys are in the school cricket team?
   c) How many boys are in the school athletics team?
   d) How many boys are in both the cricket team and in the athletics team?
   e) How many boys are not in the cricket team?
   f) How many boys are not in the athletics team?
   g) How many boys are in neither the cricket team nor in the athletics team?
   h) How many boys are in the cricket team but not in the athletics team?
   i) How many boys are in the athletics team but not in the cricket team?

&

4. The Venn diagram on the left shows the number of elements in each of the subsets of the universal set & where:
   & = {girls in class 2C}; A = {girls who take cookery};
   B = {girls who take needlework}
   a) How many girls are there in class 2C?
   b) How many girls take cookery?
   c) How many girls take needlework?
   d) How many girls take both cookery and needlework?
   e) How many girls do not take cookery?
   f) How many girls do not take needlework?
   g) How many girls do not take cookery or needlework?
   h) How many girls take cookery but not needlework?
   i) How many girls take needlework but not cookery?

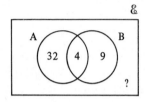

5. The Venn diagram on the left shows the number of elements in each of the subsets of the universal set & where:
& = {members of the cricket club} ; A = {members who can bowl} ;
B = {members who can keep wicket}

How many members
a) can bowl?   b) can keep wicket?
c) can bowl and keep wicket?
d) can neither bowl nor keep wicket if the club has 20 members altogether?

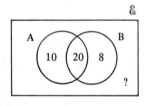

6. The Venn diagram on the left shows the number of elements in each of the subsets of the universal set & where:
& = {members of a working mens' club} ; A = {members who smoke cigarettes} ;
B = {members who smoke cigars}

How many members
a) smoke cigarettes?   b) smoke cigars?
c) smoke both cigarettes and cigars?
d) do not smoke cigarettes or cigars if the club has 50 members altogether?

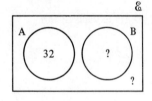

7. The Venn diagram on the left shows the number of elements in each of the subsets of the universal set & where:
& = {houses in West Street} ; A = {houses to which a morning paper is delivered} ;
B = {houses to which an evening paper is delivered}

To how many houses is
a) a morning paper delivered?   b) an evening paper delivered?
c) both a morning paper and an evening paper delivered?
d) neither a morning paper nor an evening paper delivered if there are 40 houses in the street?

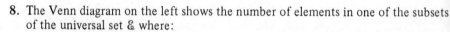

8. The Venn diagram on the left shows the number of elements in one of the subsets of the universal set & where:
& = {passengers on an overcrowded bus} ; A = {passengers sitting downstairs} ;
B = {passengers sitting upstairs}

a) How many passengers are sitting upstairs if there are three more than downstairs?
b) How many passengers are standing if there are one-quarter as many as those sitting downstairs?
c) How many passengers are travelling on the bus altogether?

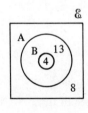

9. The Venn diagram on the left shows the number of elements in each of the subsets of the universal set & where:
& = {members of a football club} ; A = {members who played in a cup contest} ;
B = {members who scored in the same cup contest}

a) How many members played in the cup contest?
b) How many members did not play in the cup contest?
c) How many members are there in the club altogether?

10. The Venn diagram on the left shows the number of elements in each of the subsets of the universal set & where:
& = {days in a three-month period} ; A = {wet days} ;
B = {days when there was a thunderstorm}

a) How many days were wet?
b) How many days were dry if the three-month period was from January to March 1981?

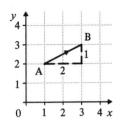

In the graph on the left, the move from A to B is 2 units to the right and 1 unit upwards.

This change of position, which has distance and direction, is called a *vector*.

The vector can be written $\overrightarrow{AB}$, or **a**; it can also be written as the column vector $\begin{pmatrix} 2 \\ 1 \end{pmatrix}$, using the grid reference. Here, the upper figure gives the distance moved to the right; the lower figure gives the displacement upwards.

Example 1

Write a column vector to describe each of the following displacements.

a) 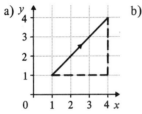 b) 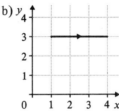 c)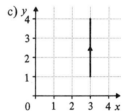

a) $\overrightarrow{XY} = \begin{pmatrix} 3 \\ 3 \end{pmatrix}$; the displacement is 3 units to the right and 3 units upwards.

b) $\overrightarrow{PQ} = \begin{pmatrix} 3 \\ 0 \end{pmatrix}$; the displacement is 3 units to the right and 0 units upwards.

c) $\overrightarrow{AB} = \begin{pmatrix} 0 \\ 3 \end{pmatrix}$; the displacement is 0 units to the right and 3 units upwards.

Exercise 63

In questions **1** to **12**, write a column vector to describe each displacement.

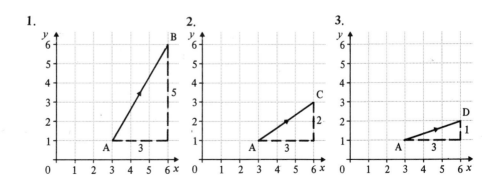

4.

5.

6.

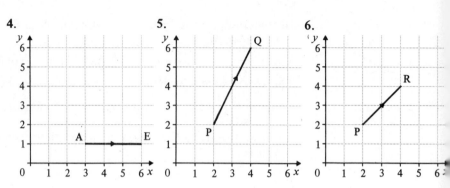

7.

8.

9.

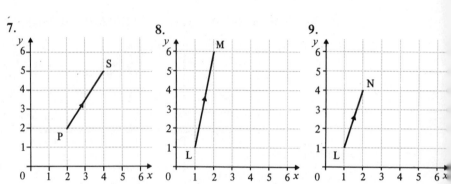

10.

11.

12.

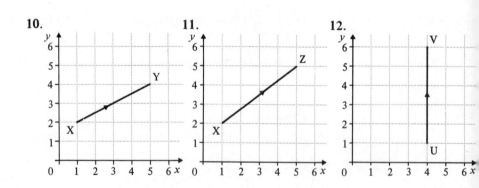

For each of questions **13** to **24**, copy the grid shown on the right. Then draw the displacement described by each column vector.

13. $\overrightarrow{AB} = \begin{pmatrix} 3 \\ 1 \end{pmatrix}$ **14.** $\overrightarrow{AC} = \begin{pmatrix} 3 \\ 3 \end{pmatrix}$ **15.** $\overrightarrow{AD} = \begin{pmatrix} 2 \\ 5 \end{pmatrix}$

16. $\overrightarrow{AE} = \begin{pmatrix} 2 \\ 1 \end{pmatrix}$ **17.** $\overrightarrow{AF} = \begin{pmatrix} 2 \\ 0 \end{pmatrix}$ **18.** $\overrightarrow{AG} = \begin{pmatrix} 4 \\ 1 \end{pmatrix}$

19. $\overrightarrow{AH} = \begin{pmatrix} 4 \\ 4 \end{pmatrix}$ **20.** $\overrightarrow{AI} = \begin{pmatrix} 4 \\ 0 \end{pmatrix}$ **21.** $\overrightarrow{AJ} = \begin{pmatrix} 1 \\ 4 \end{pmatrix}$

22. $\overrightarrow{AK} = \begin{pmatrix} 1 \\ 2 \end{pmatrix}$ **23.** $\overrightarrow{AL} = \begin{pmatrix} 0 \\ 4 \end{pmatrix}$ **24.** $\overrightarrow{AM} = \begin{pmatrix} 0 \\ 1 \end{pmatrix}$

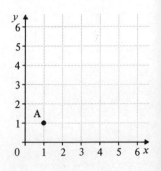

Example 2

Write a column vector to describe each of the following displacements.

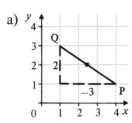 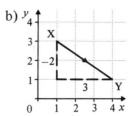 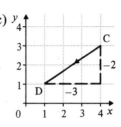

a) $\overrightarrow{PQ} = \begin{pmatrix} -3 \\ 2 \end{pmatrix}$; the displacement is 3 units to the left and 2 units upwards.

b) $\overrightarrow{XY} = \begin{pmatrix} 3 \\ -2 \end{pmatrix}$; the displacement is 3 units to the right and 2 units downwards.

c) $\overrightarrow{CD} = \begin{pmatrix} -3 \\ -2 \end{pmatrix}$; the displacement is 3 units to the left and 2 units downwards.

Exercise 64

In questions **1** to **12**, write a column vector to describe each displacement.

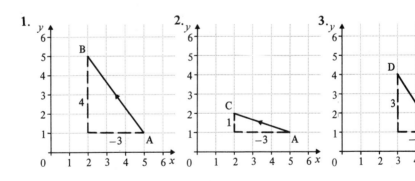

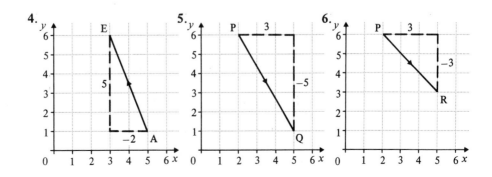

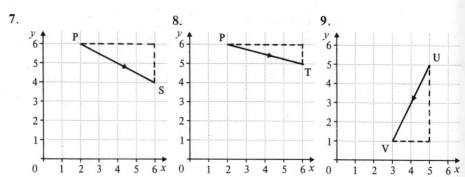

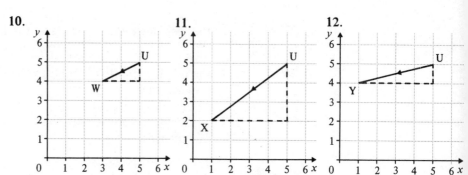

For each of questions **13** to **16**, copy the grid shown on the right. Then draw the displacement described by each column vector.

13. $\overrightarrow{AB} = \begin{pmatrix} -3 \\ 5 \end{pmatrix}$ **14.** $\overrightarrow{AC} = \begin{pmatrix} -3 \\ 3 \end{pmatrix}$ **15.** $\overrightarrow{AD} = \begin{pmatrix} -2 \\ 4 \end{pmatrix}$

16. $\overrightarrow{AE} = \begin{pmatrix} -2 \\ 1 \end{pmatrix}$

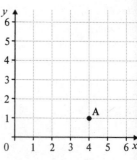

For each of questions **17** to **20**, copy the grid shown on the right. Then draw the displacement described by each column vector.

17. $\overrightarrow{PT} = \begin{pmatrix} 3 \\ -4 \end{pmatrix}$ **18.** $\overrightarrow{PR} = \begin{pmatrix} 3 \\ -1 \end{pmatrix}$ **19.** $\overrightarrow{PS} = \begin{pmatrix} 4 \\ -5 \end{pmatrix}$

20. $\overrightarrow{PT} = \begin{pmatrix} 4 \\ -3 \end{pmatrix}$

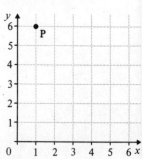

For each of questions **21** to **24**, copy the grid shown on the right. Then draw the displacement described by each column vector.

21. $\overrightarrow{UV} = \begin{pmatrix} -2 \\ -3 \end{pmatrix}$ **22.** $\overrightarrow{UW} = \begin{pmatrix} -2 \\ -5 \end{pmatrix}$ **23.** $\overrightarrow{UX} = \begin{pmatrix} -4 \\ -2 \end{pmatrix}$

24. $\overrightarrow{UY} = \begin{pmatrix} -4 \\ -5 \end{pmatrix}$

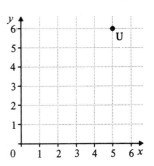

Two or more vectors can be combined to give a resultant vector. In the graph on the left

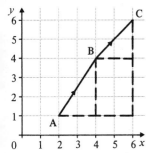

$$\overrightarrow{AB} = \begin{pmatrix} 2 \\ 3 \end{pmatrix} \text{ and } \overrightarrow{BC} = \begin{pmatrix} 2 \\ 2 \end{pmatrix}$$

$$\text{So } \overrightarrow{AC} = \overrightarrow{AB} + \overrightarrow{BC} = \begin{pmatrix} 2 \\ 3 \end{pmatrix} + \begin{pmatrix} 2 \\ 2 \end{pmatrix} = \begin{pmatrix} 4 \\ 5 \end{pmatrix}$$

Example 3

Give a single vector to describe the following displacements.

a) $\overrightarrow{AC}$ where $\overrightarrow{AB} = \begin{pmatrix} 2 \\ 1 \end{pmatrix}$ and $\overrightarrow{BC} = \begin{pmatrix} 1 \\ 1 \end{pmatrix}$

b) $\overrightarrow{XZ}$ where $\overrightarrow{XY} = \begin{pmatrix} 2 \\ 2 \end{pmatrix}$ and $\overrightarrow{YZ} = \begin{pmatrix} -3 \\ 1 \end{pmatrix}$

a) $\overrightarrow{AC} = \overrightarrow{AB} + \overrightarrow{AC} = \begin{pmatrix} 2 \\ 1 \end{pmatrix} + \begin{pmatrix} 1 \\ 1 \end{pmatrix} = \begin{pmatrix} 3 \\ 2 \end{pmatrix}$

This is shown in graph a) on the left.

b) $\overrightarrow{XZ} = \overrightarrow{XY} + \overrightarrow{YZ} = \begin{pmatrix} 2 \\ 2 \end{pmatrix} + \begin{pmatrix} -3 \\ 1 \end{pmatrix} = \begin{pmatrix} -1 \\ 3 \end{pmatrix}$

This is shown in graph b) on the left.

a)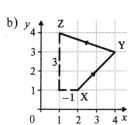

Exercise 65

Give a single vector to describe each of the following displacements.

1. $\overrightarrow{AC}$, where $\overrightarrow{AB} = \begin{pmatrix} 3 \\ 2 \end{pmatrix}$ and $\overrightarrow{BC} = \begin{pmatrix} 2 \\ 4 \end{pmatrix}$

2. $\overrightarrow{AC}$, where $\overrightarrow{AB} = \begin{pmatrix} 4 \\ 1 \end{pmatrix}$ and $\overrightarrow{BC} = \begin{pmatrix} 2 \\ 3 \end{pmatrix}$

3. $\overrightarrow{PR}$, where $\overrightarrow{PQ} = \begin{pmatrix} 5 \\ 2 \end{pmatrix}$ and $\overrightarrow{QR} = \begin{pmatrix} 3 \\ 3 \end{pmatrix}$

4. $\overrightarrow{XZ}$, where $\overrightarrow{XY} = \begin{pmatrix} 4 \\ 3 \end{pmatrix}$ and $\overrightarrow{YZ} = \begin{pmatrix} 3 \\ -2 \end{pmatrix}$

5. $\overrightarrow{UW}$, where $\overrightarrow{UV} = \begin{pmatrix} 2 \\ 5 \end{pmatrix}$ and $\overrightarrow{VW} = \begin{pmatrix} 4 \\ -3 \end{pmatrix}$

6. $\overrightarrow{LN}$, where $\overrightarrow{LM} = \begin{pmatrix} 4 \\ 2 \end{pmatrix}$ and $\overrightarrow{MN} = \begin{pmatrix} 5 \\ -1 \end{pmatrix}$

7. $\overrightarrow{AC}$, where $\overrightarrow{AB} = \begin{pmatrix} 2 \\ 3 \end{pmatrix}$ and $\overrightarrow{BC} = \begin{pmatrix} 3 \\ -5 \end{pmatrix}$

8. $\overrightarrow{RT}$, where $\overrightarrow{RS} = \begin{pmatrix} 3 \\ 1 \end{pmatrix}$ and $\overrightarrow{ST} = \begin{pmatrix} 1 \\ -4 \end{pmatrix}$

9. $\overrightarrow{XZ}$, where $\overrightarrow{XY} = \begin{pmatrix} 5 \\ 2 \end{pmatrix}$ and $\overrightarrow{YZ} = \begin{pmatrix} -3 \\ 1 \end{pmatrix}$

10. $\overrightarrow{BD}$, where $\overrightarrow{BC} = \begin{pmatrix} 3 \\ 4 \end{pmatrix}$ and $\overrightarrow{CD} = \begin{pmatrix} -2 \\ 2 \end{pmatrix}$

11. $\overrightarrow{LN}$, where $\overrightarrow{LM} = \begin{pmatrix} 2 \\ 3 \end{pmatrix}$ and $\overrightarrow{MN} = \begin{pmatrix} -4 \\ 2 \end{pmatrix}$

12. $\overrightarrow{PR}$, where $\overrightarrow{PQ} = \begin{pmatrix} 1 \\ 2 \end{pmatrix}$ and $\overrightarrow{QR} = \begin{pmatrix} -5 \\ 4 \end{pmatrix}$

13. $\overrightarrow{UW}$, where $\overrightarrow{UV} = \begin{pmatrix} 5 \\ 4 \end{pmatrix}$ and $\overrightarrow{VW} = \begin{pmatrix} -3 \\ -1 \end{pmatrix}$

14. $\overrightarrow{XZ}$, where $\overrightarrow{XY} = \begin{pmatrix} 6 \\ 3 \end{pmatrix}$ and $\overrightarrow{YZ} = \begin{pmatrix} -3 \\ -2 \end{pmatrix}$

15. $\overrightarrow{RT}$, where $\overrightarrow{RS} = \begin{pmatrix} 2 \\ 4 \end{pmatrix}$ and $\overrightarrow{ST} = \begin{pmatrix} -5 \\ -6 \end{pmatrix}$

16. $\overrightarrow{BD}$, where $\overrightarrow{BC} = \begin{pmatrix} 3 \\ 2 \end{pmatrix}$ and $\overrightarrow{CD} = \begin{pmatrix} -4 \\ -6 \end{pmatrix}$

17. $\overrightarrow{PR}$, where $\overrightarrow{PQ} = \begin{pmatrix} 3 \\ 4 \end{pmatrix}$ and $\overrightarrow{QR} = \begin{pmatrix} -1 \\ -7 \end{pmatrix}$

18. $\overrightarrow{UW}$, where $\overrightarrow{UV} = \begin{pmatrix} 5 \\ 1 \end{pmatrix}$ and $\overrightarrow{VW} = \begin{pmatrix} -2 \\ -3 \end{pmatrix}$

19. $\overrightarrow{AC}$, where $\overrightarrow{AB} = \begin{pmatrix} 4 \\ 3 \end{pmatrix}$ and $\overrightarrow{BC} = \begin{pmatrix} -8 \\ -2 \end{pmatrix}$

20. $\overrightarrow{XZ}$, where $\overrightarrow{XY} = \begin{pmatrix} 5 \\ 6 \end{pmatrix}$ and $\overrightarrow{YZ} = \begin{pmatrix} -6 \\ -4 \end{pmatrix}$

Exercise 66

A map of a boating lake is shown below. The map has a grid of 50 metre squares.

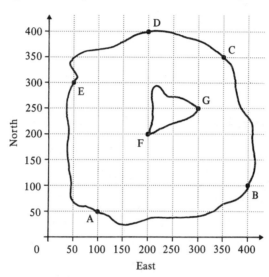

Write a column vector to describe each movement of a boat between the points
given below.

1. $\overrightarrow{AF}$	2. $\overrightarrow{GC}$	3. $\overrightarrow{EA}$	4. $\overrightarrow{EF}$
5. $\overrightarrow{DC}$	6. $\overrightarrow{GD}$	7. $\overrightarrow{BF}$	8. $\overrightarrow{BG}$
9. $\overrightarrow{DE}$	10. $\overrightarrow{DA}$	11. $\overrightarrow{AF} + \overrightarrow{FD}$	12. $\overrightarrow{ED} + \overrightarrow{DC}$
13. $\overrightarrow{AF} + \overrightarrow{FB}$	14. $\overrightarrow{ED} + \overrightarrow{DG}$	15. $\overrightarrow{GC} + \overrightarrow{CB}$	16. $\overrightarrow{FD} + \overrightarrow{DB}$
17. $\overrightarrow{GC} + \overrightarrow{CD}$	18. $\overrightarrow{AF} + \overrightarrow{FE}$	19. $\overrightarrow{ED} + \overrightarrow{DA}$	20. $\overrightarrow{GC} + \overrightarrow{CE}$

Example 4

If $\mathbf{a} = \begin{pmatrix} 2 \\ 1 \end{pmatrix}$, $\mathbf{b} = \begin{pmatrix} -3 \\ 1 \end{pmatrix}$, and $\mathbf{c} = \begin{pmatrix} -2 \\ -3 \end{pmatrix}$, find the resultant vectors for
the following

a) $\mathbf{a} + \mathbf{b}$ b) $3\mathbf{c}$ c) $\mathbf{c} - \mathbf{a}$ d) $\mathbf{a} + \mathbf{b} - \mathbf{c}$

a) $\mathbf{a} + \mathbf{b} = \begin{pmatrix} 2 \\ 1 \end{pmatrix} + \begin{pmatrix} -3 \\ 1 \end{pmatrix} = \begin{pmatrix} 2 + -3 \\ 1 + 1 \end{pmatrix} = \begin{pmatrix} -1 \\ 2 \end{pmatrix}$

b) $3c = 3\begin{pmatrix} -2 \\ -3 \end{pmatrix} = \begin{pmatrix} 3 \times -2 \\ 3 \times -3 \end{pmatrix} = \begin{pmatrix} -6 \\ -9 \end{pmatrix}$

c) $c - a = \begin{pmatrix} -2 \\ -3 \end{pmatrix} - \begin{pmatrix} 2 \\ 1 \end{pmatrix} = \begin{pmatrix} -2 - 2 \\ -3 - 1 \end{pmatrix} = \begin{pmatrix} -4 \\ -4 \end{pmatrix}$

d) $a + b - c = \begin{pmatrix} 2 \\ 1 \end{pmatrix} + \begin{pmatrix} -3 \\ 1 \end{pmatrix} - \begin{pmatrix} -2 \\ -3 \end{pmatrix} = \begin{pmatrix} 2 + -3 \\ 1 + 1 \end{pmatrix} - \begin{pmatrix} -2 \\ -3 \end{pmatrix}$

$$= \begin{pmatrix} -1 \\ +2 \end{pmatrix} - \begin{pmatrix} -2 \\ -3 \end{pmatrix}$$

$$= \begin{pmatrix} -1 - -2 \\ +2 - -3 \end{pmatrix}$$

$$= \begin{pmatrix} -1 + 2 \\ +2 + 3 \end{pmatrix} = \begin{pmatrix} 1 \\ 5 \end{pmatrix}$$

Exercise 67

1. If $a = \begin{pmatrix} 3 \\ 2 \end{pmatrix}$, $b = \begin{pmatrix} 4 \\ 2 \end{pmatrix}$ and $c = \begin{pmatrix} 5 \\ 3 \end{pmatrix}$, find the resultant vectors for the following:

   a) $a + b$ b) $c - a$ c) $a + b - c$ d) $4a$

2. If $p = \begin{pmatrix} 1 \\ 3 \end{pmatrix}$, $q = \begin{pmatrix} 5 \\ 2 \end{pmatrix}$ and $r = \begin{pmatrix} 4 \\ 4 \end{pmatrix}$, find the resultant vectors for the following:

   a) $p + q$ b) $r - p$ c) $p + q - r$ d) $3p$

3. If $x = \begin{pmatrix} 4 \\ 2 \end{pmatrix}$, $y = \begin{pmatrix} 2 \\ -5 \end{pmatrix}$ and $z = \begin{pmatrix} 5 \\ 1 \end{pmatrix}$, find the resultant vectors for the following:

   a) $x + y$ b) $z - x$ c) $x + y + z$ d) $2y$

4. If $t = \begin{pmatrix} 2 \\ 4 \end{pmatrix}$, $u = \begin{pmatrix} 4 \\ -6 \end{pmatrix}$ and $v = \begin{pmatrix} 6 \\ 1 \end{pmatrix}$, find the resultant vectors for the following:

   a) $t + u$ b) $v - t$ c) $t + u + v$ d) $5u$

5. If $a = \begin{pmatrix} 3 \\ 2 \end{pmatrix}$, $b = \begin{pmatrix} -5 \\ 4 \end{pmatrix}$ and $c = \begin{pmatrix} 1 \\ 5 \end{pmatrix}$, find the resultant vectors for the following:

   a) $a + b$ b) $c - a$ c) $a + b - c$ d) $4c + b$

6. If $r = \begin{pmatrix} 2 \\ 5 \end{pmatrix}$, $s = \begin{pmatrix} -6 \\ 2 \end{pmatrix}$ and $t = \begin{pmatrix} 0 \\ 8 \end{pmatrix}$, find the resultant vectors for the following:

   a) $r + s$ b) $t - r$ c) $r + s - t$ d) $2s + r$

7. If $x = \begin{pmatrix} 2 \\ 3 \end{pmatrix}$, $y = \begin{pmatrix} -4 \\ -5 \end{pmatrix}$ and $z = \begin{pmatrix} 1 \\ 0 \end{pmatrix}$, find the resultant vectors for the following:

   a) $x + y$ b) $z - x$ c) $x + y - z$ d) $2y - x$

8. If $p = \begin{pmatrix} 3 \\ 1 \end{pmatrix}$, $q = \begin{pmatrix} -6 \\ -4 \end{pmatrix}$ and $r = \begin{pmatrix} -5 \\ -3 \end{pmatrix}$, find the resultant vectors for the following

   a) $p + q$ b) $r - p$ c) $r - q$ d) $p + q - r$

If a die is thrown, the set of the six possible scores is {1, 2, 3, 4, 5, 6}. The likelihood that any particular number is thrown (for example, 4) is 1 out of 6.

Example 1

Five counters, numbered 1, 2, 3, 4 and 5, are placed in a bag, what is the likelihood that the number on the counter is:

a) 4?   b) an even number?
c) a prime number?

a) The likelihood is 1 out of 5 that 4 is the number on the chosen counter.
b) There are two even numbers (2 and 4) and so the likelihood is 2 out of 5.
c) There are three prime numbers (2, 3 and 5) and so the likelihood is 3 out of 5.

Exercise 68

1. Five counters, numbered 1, 2, 3, 4 and 5, are placed in a bag. If a counter is taken from the bag, find the likelihood that the number on the counter is:
a) 2   b) 5,   c) an odd number,
d) a square number,   e) a triangular number.

2. Five counters, lettered A, B, C, D and E, are placed in a bag. If a counter is taken from the bag, find the likelihood that the letter on the counter is:
a) C,   b) E,   c) a vowel,   d) a consonant.

3. A 1p coin, a 2p coin, a 5p coin, a 10p coin and a 50p coin are placed in a bag together. If a coin is taken from the bag what is the likelihood that it will be:
a) a 1p coin?   b) a 10p coin?
c) a copper coin?   d) a silver coin?

4. There are 7 packets of crisps on a supermarket shelf: 2 are salt and vinegar, 3 are cheese and onion, and 2 are plain. If any bag is picked from the shelf, what is the likelihood that it will contain:
a) salt and vinegar crisps?
b) cheese and onion crisps?
c) plain crisps?
d) flavoured crisps of any kind?

5. Each day of the week is written on a card and the seven cards are then placed in a bag. If one of the cards is then removed from the bag, what is the likelihood that:
a) the first letter on the card is T?
b) the first letter on the card is S?
c) the card has six letters written on it?
d) the card has eight letters written on it?

The *probability* of throwing a 5 with one dice is $\frac{1}{6}$,

where $\frac{1}{6} = \dfrac{\text{the number of ways of throwing a 5}}{\text{the total number of possible scores}}$

The probability of dealing an ace from a pack of 52 cards is $\frac{4}{52} = \frac{1}{13}$,

where 4 is the number of possible successes (i.e. the number of aces in the pack) and 52 is the total number of possible outcomes. (i.e. the total number of cards in the pack)

Hence the probability of an event happening is equal to:

$$\frac{\text{number of 'successes'}}{\text{total number of possible outcomes}}$$

Example 2

If a letter is chosen at random from the word ALGEBRA, what is the probability that it will be:

a) the letter E?   b) the letter A?
c) a consonant (i.e. not a vowel)?

a) Number of 'successes', i.e. the number of E's = 1
Total number of possible outcomes, i.e. the total number of letters = 7
therefore the probability = $\frac{1}{7}$.

b) Number of 'successes' = 2
Total number of possible outcomes = 7
therefore the probability = $\frac{2}{7}$.

c) Number of 'successes' (i.e. the letters L, G, B and R) = 4
Total number of possible outcomes = 7
therefore the probability = $\frac{4}{7}$.

Exercise 69

1. If a letter is chosen at random from the word
   SUCCESS, what is the probability that it will be:
   a) the letter S?   b) the letter C?

2. If a letter is chosen at random from the word
   PEPPER, what is the probability that it will be:
   a) the letter P?   b) the letter E?

3. If a letter is chosen at random from the name
   GEORGE, what is the probability that it will be:
   a) the letter E?   b) the letter G?
   c) a vowel?   d) a consonant?

4. If a letter is chosen at random from the name
   PENELOPE, what is the probability that it will
   be:
   a) the letter E?   b) the letter P?
   c) a vowel?   d) a consonant?

5. If a letter is chosen at random from the word
   WOODWORK, what is the probability that it will
   be:
   a) the letter O?   b) the letter W?
   c) a consonant?

6. If a letter is chosen at random from the word
   NEEDLEWORK, what is the probability that it
   will be:
   a) the letter E?   b) a vowel?
   c) a consonant?

7. On a supermarket shelf there are 16 bags of sugar,
   12 of which contain white sugar and 4 of which
   contain brown sugar. If a bag is taken at random,
   what is the probability that it will contain:
   a) white sugar?   b) brown sugar?

8. In class 3A there are 12 boys and 8 girls. If the
   pupils leave their classroom and walk to the
   assembly hall in any random order, what it is the
   probability that the first pupil to enter the hall
   will be:
   a) a boy?   b) a girl?

9. A farmer has 25 white sheep and 5 black sheep.
   If they are rounded up for shearing in any random
   order, what is the probability that the first one to
   be sheared will be:
   a) white?   b) black?

10. A box of sweets contains 15 chocolates, 9 toffees
    and 6 nougats. If a sweet is taken from the box at
    random, what is the probability that it will be:
    a) a chocolate?   b) a toffee?   c) a nougat?

11. In class 2B there are 18 girls with dark hair, 10
    girls with fair hair and 2 girls with red hair. If their
    teacher asks one girl at random to give out some
    books, what is the probability that she will have:
    a) dark hair?   b) fair hair?   c) red hair?

12. A £1 cash bag contains six 10p coins, four 5p
    coins, six 2p coins and eight 1p coins. If a coin
    is removed from the bag, what is the probability
    that it will be:
    a) a 10p coin?   b) a 5p coin?
    c) a 2p coin?   d) a 1p coin?
    e) a silver coin?   f) a copper coin?

13. On a supermarket shelf there are 8 packets of
    plain crisps, 5 packets of cheese and onion crisps,
    3 packets of salt and vinegar crisps and 4 packets
    of smoky bacon crisps. If a bag is removed from
    the shelf at random, what is the probability that
    it will contain:
    a) plain crisps?
    b) cheese and onion crisps?
    c) salt and vinegar crisps?
    d) smoky bacon crisps?
    e) any kind of flavoured crisps?

14. If a dice is thrown, what is the probability that
    the score will be:
    a) a six?   b) an odd number?
    c) an even number?   d) a multiple of 3?
    e) a prime number?   f) a square number?
    g) a triangular number?

15. Twelve counters numbered 1, 2, 3, 4, 5, 6, 7, 8,
    9, 10, 11 and 12 are placed in a bag. If a counter
    is removed from the bag, what is the probability
    that the number on it will be:
    a) a prime number?   b) a square number?
    c) a triangular number?   d) a multiple of 3?
    e) a multiple of 5?

16. Twelve counters lettered A, B, C, D, E, F, G, H, I,
    J, K and L are placed in a bag. If a counter is
    removed from the bag, what is the probability
    that the letter on it will be:
    a) a vowel?   b) a consonant?
    c) any letter of the word CAGE?
    d) any letter of the word BLEACH?

17. Each month of the year is written on a card and
    the twelve cards are then placed in a bag. If one
    card is then removed from the bag, what is the
    probability that:
    a) the first letter on the card is J?
    b) the first letter on the card is M?
    c) the first letter on the card is A?
    d) the last letter on the card is R?
    e) the last letter on the card is Y?
    f) the month written on the card has 30 days?
    g) the month written on the card has 31 days?

18. Certain geometrical shapes are drawn on cards as shown and the eight cards are then placed in a bag.

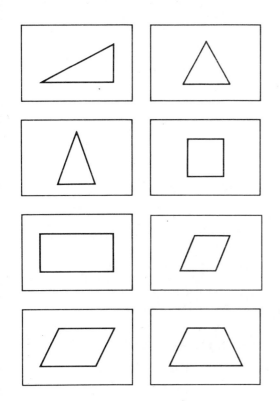

If a card is then removed from the bag, what is the probability that the figure on it has:
a) three sides?   b) four sides?
c) four equal sides?   d) all its sides equal?
e) two pairs of equal sides?
f) one pair of equal sides?

19. A bag contains 40 counters, 8 of which are red, 12 of which are yellow, 4 of which are green and 16 of which are blue. If a counter is removed from the bag, what is the probability that it is:
a) a red?   b) yellow?   c) green?   d) blue?
e) red or yellow?   f) red or green?
g) red or blue?

20. A pack of 52 playing cards is shuffled thoroughly and a card is then removed. What is the probability that the card:
a) is an ace?
b) is any king, queen or jack?
c) shows any number from 2 to 10?
d) shows any even number?
e) shows any odd number?

If a bag contains 7 yellow counters the probability of picking out a yellow counter is $\frac{7}{7}$ or 1.
Thus, the probability of a 'certainty' is 1.

Example 3

a) A case contains only pens and pencils. If the probability of picking out a pen is $\frac{3}{8}$, what is the probability of picking out a pencil?

The probability of picking a pen or a pencil (i.e. a certainty) = 1.

The probability of picking a pen = $\frac{3}{8}$;

so the probability of picking a pencil is

$$1 - \frac{3}{8} = \frac{5}{8}.$$

b) A bag contains only red, white and blue counters. If the probability of picking out a red counter is $\frac{1}{2}$ and the probability of picking out a white counter is $\frac{1}{3}$, what is the probability of picking out a blue counter?

The probability of picking a red, white or blue counter (i.e. a certainty) = 1

The probability of picking a red or a white counter (i.e. *not* a blue one) is:

$$\frac{1}{2} + \frac{1}{3} = \frac{3 + 2}{6} = \frac{5}{6}$$

Therefore the probability of picking a blue counter is:

$$1 - \frac{5}{6} = \frac{1}{6}.$$

Exercise 70

1. On a shelf in a supermarket there are bags of plain and self-raising flour. If the probability of picking a packet of plain flour is $\frac{3}{10}$, what is the probability of picking a packet of self-raising flour?
2. On another shelf in the same supermarket there are cartons of brown eggs and white eggs. If the probability of picking a carton of brown eggs is $\frac{9}{20}$, what is the probability of picking a carton of white eggs?

3. A box contains hard-and soft-centred chocolates. If the probability of picking a hard-centred chocolate is $\frac{5}{12}$, what is the probability of picking a soft-centred one?

4. When the boys in class 5A walk from their classroom to the assembly hall, there is a probability of $\frac{1}{6}$ that the first boy into the hall is one who does wear spectacles. What is the probability that the first boy into the hall does *not* wear spectacles?

5. The boys in class 1B have dark eyes, blue eyes, or green eyes. If the teacher picks any boy to give out some books, there is a probability of $\frac{1}{2}$ that he has dark eyes and a probability of $\frac{2}{5}$ that he has blue eyes. What is the probability that he has green eyes?

6. The girls in class 2C wear shoes of sizes 2, 3, or 4. If the teacher sends any girl to collect the class register, there is a probability of $\frac{1}{2}$ that she wears size 2 shoes and a probability of $\frac{3}{10}$ that she wears size 3 shoes. What is the probability that she wears size 4 shoes?

7. A £5 cash bag contains only 50p, 10p and 5p coins. If a coin is removed from the bag, there is

a probability of $\frac{1}{2}$ that it is a 5p coin and a probability of $\frac{3}{8}$ that it is a 10p coin. What is the probability that it is a 50p coin? Can you find out how many coins of each kind that there are in the bag?

8. A £50 cash bag contains only £10, £5, and £1 notes. If a note is removed from the bag, there is a probability of $\frac{3}{4}$ that it is a £1 note and a probability of $\frac{3}{20}$ that it is a £5 note. What is the probability that it is a £10 note? Can you find out how many notes of each kind there are in the bag?

9. A case contains only red, yellow, green, and blue crayons. If a crayon is removed from the case, there is a probability of $\frac{1}{4}$ that it is a red one, a probability of $\frac{1}{5}$ that it is a yellow one, and a probability of $\frac{3}{10}$ that it is a green one. What is the probability that it is a blue one?

10. A packet contains only orange, lemon, raspberry and blackcurrant sweets. If a sweet is removed from the packet, there is a probability of $\frac{1}{3}$ that it is orange flavoured, a probability of $\frac{1}{5}$ that it is lemon flavoured and a probability of $\frac{3}{10}$ that it is raspberry flavoured. What is the probability that it is blackcurrant flavoured?

REVISION EXERCISE E

1. The star pattern on the left below is rotated clockwise about O until A is in the position of B as shown on the right.

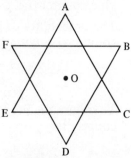 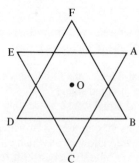

Through how many degrees has the pattern been rotated?

2. The star pattern on the left below is rotated clockwise about O until P is in the position of Q as shown on the right.

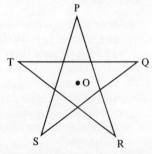 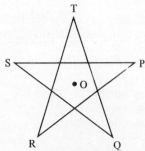

Through how many degrees has the pattern been rotated?

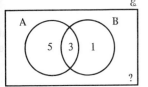

3. The Venn diagram on the left shows the number of elements in each of the subsets of the universal set & where:

   & = {the eleven players in the cricket team}
   A = {players who batted in the match}
   B = {players who bowled in the match}

How many players
a) batted?   b) bowled?
c) batted and bowled?
d) neither batted nor bowled?

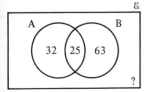

4. The Venn diagram on the left shows the number of elements in each of the subsets of the universal set & where:

   & = {passengers who travelled on the train}
   A = {passengers who had lunch on the train}
   B = {passengers who had tea on the train}

How many passengers
a) had lunch on the train?
b) had tea on the train?
c) had both lunch and tea on the train?
d) had neither meal on the train if 300 passengers travelled on the train altogether?

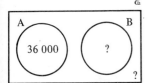

5. The Venn diagram on the left shows the number of elements in each of the subsets of the universal set & where:

   & = {people who queued at a football ground}
   A = {people who were able to stand on the terraces}
   B = {people who were able to find seats in the stand}

a) How many people found seats if there were one-eighth as many as those who stood on the terraces?
b) How many people were shut out of the ground if there were one-third as many as those sitting in the stand?
c) How many people queued at the ground altogether?

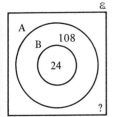

6. The Venn diagram on the left shows the number of elements in each of the subsets of the universal set & where:

   & = {the third year pupils at Willow Bank School}
   A = {pupils who obtained a pass in the English test}
   B = {pupils who obtained a credit in the same test}

How many pupils
a) passed the test?
b) failed the test if there are 150 pupils in the third year altogether?

7. If a letter is chosen at random from the word BANANA, what is the probability that it will be:
a) the letter A?   b) the letter N?   c) the letter B?

8. Each season of the year is written on a card and the four cards are then placed in a bag. If one card is then removed from the bag, what is the probability that:
a) the first letter on the card is S?
b) the last letter on the card is R?
c) there are six letters on the card?

9. Ten counters lettered M, N, O, P, Q, R, S, T, U and V are placed in a bag. If a counter is removed from the bag, what is the probability that the letter on it will be:
a) a vowel?   b) a consonent?
c) any letter of the word TOUR?
d) any letter of the word SPORT?
e) any letter of the word SPROUT?

A map of certain airports in England and Wales is shown below. The map has a gr of 50 kilometre squares.

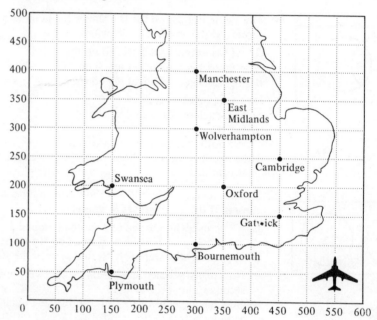

Write a column vector to describe each movement of an aeroplane between the airports given below.

10. Plymouth to Bournemouth
11. Plymouth to Wolverhampton
12. Plymouth to Manchester
13. Plymouth to Gatwick
14. Plymouth to Cambridge
15. Plymouth to Swansea
16. Manchester to East Midlands
17. Manchester to Oxford
18. Manchester to Cambridge
19. Manchester to Gatwick
20. Manchester to Wolverhampton
21. Manchester to Bournemouth
22. Gatwick to Oxford
23. Gatwick to East Midlands
24. Gatwick to Wolverhampton
25. Gatwick to Swansea
26. Gatwick to Cambridge
27. East Midlands to Wolverhampton
28. East Midlands to Bournemouth
29. East Midlands to Swansea
30. East Midlands to Plymouth